The Pledge

★

The
PLEDGE

★

A HISTORY OF THE
PLEDGE OF ALLEGIANCE

Jeffrey Owen Jones
and Peter Meyer

THOMAS DUNNE BOOKS
ST. MARTIN'S PRESS
NEW YORK

THOMAS DUNNE BOOKS.
An imprint of St. Martin's Press.

THE PLEDGE. Copyright © 2010 by Jeffrey Owen Jones and Peter Meyer.
All rights reserved. Printed in the United States of America. For information, address St. Martin's Press, 175 Fifth Avenue, New York, N.Y. 10010.

www.thomasdunnebooks.com
www.stmartins.com

ISBN 978-0-312-35002-4

First Edition: October 2010

10 9 8 7 6 5 4 3 2 1

TO JEFFREY OWEN JONES,
WHO LOVED A GOOD STORY

CONTENTS

ACKNOWLEDGMENTS

While I am, and always will be, saddened that Jeff did not live to finish this book, I feel honored to have played a role in its completion and know Jeff would have been proud of it.

I would like to thank *The Smithsonian* for publishing Jeff's article on the Pledge of Allegiance.

Many thanks to the University of Rochester Library in whose archives reside the papers of Francis Bellamy.

To John Ware, who understood, coached, and supported—many, many thanks.

To Thomas Dunne and Peter Joseph of St. Martin's Press, I thank you for picking up the reins and continuing the project. I thank you doubly for your wisdom in hiring Peter Meyer. Thanks to Peter Meyer for taking up the reins and riding (or writing) to the finish line.

I owe a debt of gratitude to Christopher and Hilda Jones. Your love and support kept this project afloat.

My thanks to Peter Richardson and Steve Atlas, who, by example, define friendship and loyalty.

My deepest personal thanks go to our Pittsford team of angels: Dr. Dave Trawick and Dr. Becky Monk, Dr. Steve Ignaczak and Dr. Judy Kramer, Dr. Steve Meyers and Dr. Barbara Weber, Dr. Margaret Donahue, and Dr. Victor and Mrs. Susan Regenbogen, Dr. T. Scott Campbell, Dr. Timothy Quill and Dr. Aaron Olden. By surrounding us with your expertise, empathy, and humanity, you kept our spirits high.

ACKNOWLEDGMENTS

Thank you to Denise DeWyn for keeping the office under control.

And thank you to our son, Eli Owen Jones, for lighting up our lives.

—ELLEN JONES

My thanks must start with Thomas Dunne, who invited me to get involved with this project; as a student of history, I jumped at the opportunity to learn about the Pledge of Allegiance, but I had no idea the subject was so rich. Of crucial help in my research were colleagues and friends Donald Christensen, Lynn Sloneker, Jacques Menasche, and Catherine Coreno—without their hugely generous and professional assistance this book would not have been possible. Also crucial to the telling of any story about the Pledge of Allegiance were the staff of the Department of Rare Books, Special Collections and Preservation at the Rush Rhees Library at the University of Rochester, where a treasure of historical documents are available (see the Bibliography); my special thanks to Rosemary Switzer and Melissa Mead at Rush Rhees. And I also reserve a special debt of gratitude to Ellen Jones, who showed so much grace and kindness in helping me gather up the files of her late husband, the author of this book. I am sorry I never met Jeffrey Owen Jones, but when I heard that he was the "Mr. Jones" in the song of my favorite poet Bob Dylan, I knew I would have liked him. And I only hope I have done some justice to Jeffrey's superbly easy and inviting writing style in finishing a project to which he devoted much personal and professional love and attention. Finally, my great thanks to Peter Joseph, an editor of immense talent and patience. And, needless to say but needful of saying, a special thanks to my wife, Janet, and son, Dylan, who put up with the many inconveniences of necessary deadlines.

—PETER MEYER

1. AN AMERICAN RITUAL

On a sultry summer evening in Boston in the year 1892, a thirty-seven-year-old former clergyman named Francis Bellamy sat down at his desk in the offices of a popular family magazine where he worked and began to write:

I pledge allegiance to my flag . . .

Neither Bellamy nor anyone else could have imagined that the single twenty-three-word sentence that emerged would evolve into one of the most familiar of patriotic texts and, based on student recitations alone, perhaps the most often repeated piece of writing in the history of the English language. A standard ritual of childhood for most native-born citizens and a regular practice for many adults, reciting the Pledge of Allegiance is so deeply embedded in American life that it is natural to believe that the text came from on high, or that it bubbled up spontaneously from the fruited plain, far back in our history. Before I heard, a few years ago, about Francis Bellamy and the writing of the Pledge, I had never stopped to think how or where it had originated. The Pledge of Allegiance had just always been there. It never occurred to me that a person had actually composed it. If I thought about the Pledge being written at all, I dimly pictured a man in a white wig with a quill pen, or a dashing figure in a ruffled shirt on the deck of a frigate, bombs bursting in air.

But no. As it turns out, the Pledge wasn't scratched on parchment in the mists of time. It came to life not that long ago, very near the beginning of the twentieth century. And the birth of the Pledge was more prosaic than heroic. It wasn't chiseled in granite or penned in blood on a battlefield. It was scribbled on scrap paper by Frank Bellamy, a guy stuck at the office on a hot summer night.

It is amusing to play historical voyeur and look back on Bellamy hunched over his desk jotting drafts on the back of an old office form. It must have seemed to him a very ordinary moment in time. There was, of course, no way for him to know that he was writing for the ages, that the words he was scribbling on deadline would spring from the lips of generations of Americans long after he was dead and gone. Never could he have conceived that in the twenty-first century multitudes of children all over the United States would begin every school day reciting his words (though somewhat altered by textual fiddling over the years). Nor could he have guessed that the flag salute he was composing— for an event that was part patriotic celebration, part promotion for the magazine that employed him—would find such a variety of uses in American life.

Today, in addition to marking the official opening of every school day for millions of students (even some homeschoolers recite it), the Pledge of Allegiance has become a ceremonial must for all occasions. Committees, councils, and legislatures— from PTAs and zoning boards to the U.S. Congress—intone the Pledge at the start of every session. Rotary, Elks, Lions, Kiwanis, Cub Scouts and Girl Scouts, American Legion, Daughters of the American Revolution (DAR), Knights of Columbus, B'nai Brith, and scores of other clubs, societies, and associations open every meeting with the Pledge. It is recited at graduations and county fair openings, at groundbreaking ceremonies and monument dedications, at professional conventions, football games, and stock car races. It is spoken in a blended chorus of accents from around the world by newly sworn American citizens. In times of war and in times of economic distress, saying the Pledge can be a kind of incantation to express solidarity and to ward off evil.

Thinking back on the evening when he wrote the Pledge, Francis Bellamy said later in life that he intended to create a vehicle for expressing "intelligent patriotism"—not only love of country but, just as important, awareness of the nation's ideals. Bellamy also said that, with the Civil War still very much in living memory and waves of immigrants arriving on American shores, he intended the phrase "one nation indivisible" (as he originally wrote it) to stand as a strong affirmation of national unity.

He would surely be pleased to see that, in today's ever more disparate society, reciting the Pledge can be a unifying ritual that bridges social and cultural divides. It is one of the few practices shared by all Americans. Yet who could have suspected that this simple flag salute would, time and again over the years, be a lightning rod for bitter controversy? That controversies over reciting the Pledge would be the focus of three U.S. Supreme Court cases and at least one other landmark appellate decision?

No doubt a former clergyman like Bellamy, whose university commencement oration was titled "The Poetry of Human Brotherhood," would be dismayed to know that American elementary-school children who refused on religious grounds to recite the Pledge in school would be expelled, their families shunned and physically attacked. That during the politically supercharged days of the 1960s, in a town not far from his birthplace in western New York State, a teacher who stood in respectful silence rather than reciting the words of the Pledge would be fired and barraged with hate mail. That a candidate for president of the United States would impugn the other candidate's patriotism because as a governor he vetoed a bill compelling teachers to lead the Pledge. That, in the twenty-first century, a municipal official in Colorado who refused to stand and recite the Pledge would lose his post in a special recall election. Or that a town in Massachusetts would divide in rancor when compulsory recitation of the Pledge would be compared by Holocaust survivors to the forced loyalty oaths of Nazi Germany.

How would the politically active Bellamy have felt if he could have looked decades ahead to see that a gaggle of pressure groups, from environmentalists to antiabortion protestors, would try to add their own ideological messages to the text of the Pledge? What would have been his position had he been alive in 1954, when the U.S. Congress added "under God" to the text, a reference to the divinity which the former clergyman himself had not included? Could he possibly have imagined that the U.S. House of Representatives would one day vote to break up the Ninth Circuit Court of Appeals because the court had ruled that having public school children recite the "under God" version of the Pledge violates the constitutional separation of church and state? Or that a sitting president would cite a commitment to preserving the "under God" Pledge in schools as a qualification for being named to the Supreme Court.

No one could have foreseen what the Pledge of Allegiance would become, the wrangles it would cause or the many ceremonial roles it would play, because there really had never been anything quite like it. The Pledge was an accident of history. It was something brand new, *sui generis,* that came to life out of a perfect coincidence of individuals and events. And nothing to match it has come along since.

What is the Pledge of Allegiance? It's a simple question, but the more I have considered it, the more challenging it is to answer. In its uses and its symbolism, as a mirror of contemporary society and historical events, the nature of the Pledge of Allegiance is rich and complex.

One of the questions people ask me most frequently about the Pledge is whether other countries have anything like it. Yes, there are popular salutes to the flag in other nations—Indonesia and Ghana among them. But nothing I have heard about anywhere else is quite like the Pledge. No salute is so deeply rooted in the national experience or so intertwined in daily life. None is so varied in its roles and as redolent with connotation.

Reciting the Pledge is a primal American experience, a constant in our lives from earliest memory. As a part of a regular routine, saying the Pledge can seem a reflexive exercise. In a larger frame, though, the Pledge is a powerful force in the national psyche. For the great majority of people born in the United States, the Pledge as a school ritual is our introduction to what it means to be an American. For many adults, an intimate link persists between the Pledge and their fundamental sense of national identity, their most fervent convictions about what the country is and ought to be.

Because its uses and associations extend so widely in contemporary America, the Pledge is pushed and pulled, squeezed and pummeled as never before. We use it as a political cudgel, an ideological bumper sticker, a vehicle of protest, a constitutional battering ram, and a judicial litmus test. Still, the Pledge lives on. In fact, it thrives. Especially since September 11, 2001, the uses of the Pledge of Allegiance have multiplied. The day after the terrorist attacks, Muslim men in beards and robes stood before cameras in Dallas, Texas, reciting the Pledge as a demonstration of their *Americanness*. One month after 9/11, then secretary of education Rod Paige urged American schoolchildren to recite the Pledge as an exercise in solidarity. On the third anniversary of the attacks, then secretary of defense Donald Rumsfeld read the Pledge at the Chevy Rock & Roll 400 NASCAR race. And in the fall of 2004, neighbors and friends of an American executed in Iraq intoned the Pledge at a candlelight vigil in his Michigan hometown. Reported the *New York Times*:

> The vigil took place in the early evening while it was still light in front of the Hillsdale County Courthouse on a town square framed by light poles bearing

hanging planters with purple flowers. The Pledge of
Allegiance was recited, candles were wedged into
plastic coffee cup lids and passed through the crowd,
and a local pastor . . . was asked to say a few words.

Everyone, it seems, has a Pledge story: how they used to
think it began "I play Joe legions"; how they one day blanked
on the words; or about the schoolmate who refused to recite it.
Lee Siskind, a businessman in Lowell, Massachusetts, told me
he remembers saying the Pledge outside his tent each morning
during a Boy Scout Jamboree at the 1939 New York World's
Fair. Art Lubetz, a Pittsburgh architect, said he recalls that his
Jewish grandmother, who escaped persecution in czarist Russia,
complained about the Pledge: "I *love* this country. I don't need
to pledge allegiance."

After Private James Prevetes was killed in Iraq in the fall of
2004, his first-grade teacher, Janice Hengle, called up a vision of
him saying the Pledge in her classroom. "He stood perfectly
straight and tall," she told a *New York Times* reporter. Raise the
Pledge as a topic at a local Lions Club meeting, as I did not long
ago, and a flood of words pours forth. Even the most taciturn
have memories to share, anecdotes to report.

My own firsthand experience with the Pledge as an adult includes two particularly memorable experiences. One occurred
a few years ago in Petersburg, Alaska, where I had gone to do
ground work for a documentary. I remember the Alaska Airlines
jetliner I had caught in Seattle descending out of a low cloud into
the half-light of a northern winter morning. Houses, boat har-
bors, and commercial buildings spread out below along a rim of
land, surrounded by muskeg and trees, mountains and water. The
cliché about Alaska as the last frontier came vividly to mind.

At the little airport terminal, Ted Smith, the mayor of Petersburg, greeted me. Mayor Smith and I drove down the town's

gravelly streets under a brightening midday sky. It was Rotary day, and the mayor had invited me to lunch.

In the low-slung Boys and Girls Club building where the Rotary Club meets, I joined a line of thirty or so men and women waiting for soup and sandwiches, which we ate at long folding tables. As lunch wound down, it was time for the business meeting, presided over by a woman in a Forest Service uniform. When she walked to the front of the room, everyone stood and prepared to recite the Pledge.

It was the first time I had said the Pledge in a public gathering in a long while. Not being a Rotarian, or a member of any of the many other groups that say the Pledge routinely, I was frankly surprised to find myself standing hand over heart, practicing a childhood ritual. But reciting the familiar phrases was somehow comforting. In this room where I was a total stranger far from home, I felt connected. The Pledge was something we had in common. Reciting it with the others made me part of the group.

Back home a few months afterward, my son Eli, then five years old, announced that he had led the Pledge of Allegiance in his kindergarten class that day.

"What was that like?" I asked. He jumped up from the living room floor and stood facing imaginary classmates.

"Please salute," he said, placing his hand over his heart. "Please begin." Beaming, he then recited the Pledge flawlessly.

I experienced that moment with what I can only describe as a feeling of genuine reverence. Eli's recitation was, I realized, a rite of passage. His learning the Pledge was a first step toward civic consciousness, toward awareness that he is part of a citizenry, that he has a flag that stands for a nation with ideals and principles. Eli was moving out of the toddler world toward the larger community of the body politic. He and I, father and son, were now connecting on a new level—as fellow citizens.

As anyone who has ever said the rosary or chanted a mantra knows, repeating words over and over tends to drain them of literal meaning. One morning when I was substitute teaching in a big suburban middle school, an outsized eighth-grade boy remained sprawled in his chair as the other students stood to say the Pledge. When I motioned to him to stand up, he gave me the adolescent look of long-suffering annoyance so familiar to parents and teachers. "Why do we have to say this every morning?" he groaned. "I already know the words." It was a good question. Why indeed?

The text of the Pledge reads as a promise of fidelity and a shorthand statement of national principles. In many contexts, though, the direct significance of the Pledge is clearly secondary to its symbolic, ceremonial function.

For school kids, beyond the patriotic promise and the evocation of high ideals, reciting the Pledge is a ritual of joint enterprise that says, this day is officially beginning now and we are going into it together. In the case of my son's first recitation, and in my experience in Alaska, the meaning of the words was secondary to the act of reciting them. Eli didn't understand the definition of *allegiance* or *republic* (who does?) or even of *the United States of America*. (He was still sorting out the basics of geography: for him, "our state" meant the entire world beyond our town.) His excitement came from standing up with his classmates, striking the ceremonial hand-over-heart pose, facing the Stars and Stripes, speaking the rhythmic text and hearing it resound around him. What happened to me in Alaska was similar. It was the feeling of unity and being at home among a group of strangers that touched me more than the ideas we were affirming.

Of course, there are many instances where the literal meaning of every word in the Pledge is important. So it was one morning in the fall of 2005 when I stopped in at the Monroe County building in downtown Rochester, New York, not far from where I live. There I found the county council chamber humming with conversations in a variety of languages. I had come to witness the monthly swearing-in of naturalized citizens in this region of the state. The information sheet I was handed said there were forty-six candidates for U.S. citizenship from thirty-one countries of the world. There were Asians, Africans, Middle Easterners, Latin Americans, and Europeans. Families and friends embraced and exchanged kisses.

The proceedings began with brief remarks from the presiding judge, who commended the participants on having worked hard to fulfill the requirements to become citizens. An official from the U.S. Bureau of Citizenship and Immigration Service next introduced the candidates as a group. Then they all raised their right hands and the county clerk read the oath of citizenship, a weighty text:

> I hereby declare, on oath, that I absolutely and
> entirely renounce and abjure all allegiance and
> fidelity to any foreign prince, potentate, state, or
> sovereignty of whom or which I have heretofore
> been a subject or citizen; that I will support and
> defend the Constitution and laws of the United
> States of America against all enemies, foreign and
> domestic . . .

After the oath, a women's a capella octet, dressed in mauve blazers with pink carnations, relieved the somber tone of the proceedings. The altos began: *thrum, thrum, thrum* . . . Then the sopranos: *Mine eyes have seen the glory of the coming of the Lord* . . . I couldn't help wondering, as they sang, how many of the new citizens were Christian. Given the moment, though, and the exuberance of the octet, no one was likely to quibble.

Next came the guest speaker, a county court judge. I braced myself for perfunctory remarks long on wind and short on inspiration. Instead, the Honorable John J. Connell spoke with emotion about how, eleven years before, he had taken the same oath on behalf of a young boy whom he and his wife had adopted from a foreign country in turmoil. "I feel privileged to be here," said Judge Connell. "This is a day to celebrate."

Then, after each new citizen had received a certificate and a small American flag, the group stood and recited in unison the Pledge of Allegiance. Except for the simple "I do" that they had said in affirmation of their naturalization oath, these were the only words the forty-six new citizens uttered during the ceremony. For many, I imagine, it was the first English-language text they had committed to memory. I am sure that, more than most of us, they savored the meaning of every word.

The text of the Pledge has been changing almost from the moment Bellamy set down the original twenty-two-word version:

> I pledge allegiance to my flag and the republic for which it stands—one nation indivisible—with liberty and justice for all.

Bellamy himself made the first edit, soon after the initial version went into print. He added "to" before "the republic" because he felt it gave the lines better cadence.

As Bellamy's flag salute became more popular, there arose a temptation to edit the text further. In the 1920s, a National Flag Commission made up of DAR ladies and American Legionnaires changed the intimate phrase "my flag" to "the flag of the United States of America." Their stated purpose was to be sure that immigrant children arriving on American shores would know which country's flag they were saluting. This change reflects the era of isolationism and mistrust of all things foreign that followed World War I. Ironically, Congress sharply reduced immigration quotas during this period, ensuring that there would be fewer children from overseas to salute the Stars and Stripes.

The most resounding change in the Pledge also reflected a national preoccupation with threats from abroad. This was the addition of "under God" in 1954.

I remember in that year being at school on a late-spring afternoon in the Connecticut town where I grew up. Itching to get outside and play kickball, I stood with hand over heart in Mrs. Sholz's fourth-grade classroom, practicing the new version of the Pledge due to take effect on Flag Day, June 14. My classmates and I kept stumbling. We were accustomed to the fluid cadence of the existing text—"one nation indivisible, with liberty and justice for all." It was hard to shake the rhythm of the old version; even the following fall a few of us would blurt out the former text in school assemblies. Eventually, though, the new Pledge became routine. Now, fewer and fewer Americans remember it any other way.

By 1954, Congress had assumed authority over the Pledge as part of the official flag code. The sponsors of the bill to insert "under God" declared that the addition would underscore the difference between our system and "Godless communism." World War II was less than a decade in the past, and the allied commanding general was now in the White House. The Soviet Union and Red China were the new threats. Anticommunism had become a national obsession, and vestiges of the paranoia stoked by Senator Joseph McCarthy still lingered.

In Congress, there was little opposition. At the time, American culture had a more homogeneous feel than it does today. White Christian values and images predominated in the media and in popular culture. There was little popular sensitivity to practitioners of Buddhism, Hinduism, or other religions that did not embrace the concept of a single deity—let alone to nonbelievers.

Naturally, there were many individual citizens who objected to altering a text that had served the country through two world wars and the Great Depression. Judy Hyman, who was raised on the Upper West Side of Manhattan, remembers that her father, Bruno Giordano Shaw, was furious. An atheist named for the Renaissance philosopher Giordano Bruno, who was burned at the stake for heresy, Bruno Shaw would rail against the addition of "under God" to anyone who would listen. Such personal protests continue to this day. My friend Kevin Kelly, a psychiatrist in New York City, wrote this in an e-mail message:

> As an unregenerate child of the '60s, I object to the Pledge even without a deity in it, because it seems to me that if you believe in the ideals for which "the Republic for which it stands" stands, you won't want to force anyone to pledge allegiance.

Some people protest by abstaining from saying the Pledge. Others simply fall silent when the phrase "under God" comes along. One man, Billiam Vanroestenberg of Plattekill, New York, stopped saying "under God" because he found it a contradiction. Vanroestenberg told the Associated Press that he regularly omitted the phrase when reciting the Pledge at his local zoning board meeting because he felt that a nation truly under God would not discriminate against gay people, like himself. Then, in March 2004, Mr. Vanroestenberg and his partner were married by the mayor of New Paltz, New York. At the next zoning meeting, he resumed saying "under God." "They all sort of applauded afterward," he said.

It was as if Abraham Lincoln had entered the room. The president who saved the Union had inherited the founders' firm belief in what E. D. Hirsch has called "a religious devotion to democracy." And he seemed to foretell Vanroestenberg's sudden change of heart about the "under God" phrase once the law was changed. Said Lincoln, in his famous 1838 Lyceum speech, called "The Perpetuation of Our Political Institutions":

> Let reverence for the laws, be breathed by every American mother, to the lisping babe, that prattles on her lap—let it be taught in schools, in seminaries, and in colleges;—let it be written in Primers, spell- ing books, and in Almanacs;—let it be preached from the pulpit, proclaimed in legislative halls, and en- forced in courts of justice. And, in short, let it be- come the political religion of the nation; and let the old and the young, the rich and the poor, the grave and the gay, of all sexes and tongues, and colors and conditions, sacrifice unceasingly upon its altars.

It's unlikely that Lincoln's understanding of "gay" would cor- respond to that of Mr. Vanroestenberg, but no doubt the two men, separated by almost two centuries, share a near religious devotion to democracy.

What turned out to be the loudest "under God" protest to date came in the year 2000 from Michael Newdow, an atheist who filed suit alleging that recitation of the Pledge of Alle- giance in his daughter's California public school violated the constitutional separation of church and state. Even though his daughter had the right to opt out of saying the Pledge, Newdow argued that school recitation of the "under God" Pledge sent an officially sanctioned message to his daughter that conflicted with his own religious tenets as a nonbeliever.

The case found its way to the U.S. Court of Appeals for the Ninth Circuit, and in 2002 the court issued a surprise ruling in Newdow's favor. The opinion set off shockwaves of anger and disbelief. In Washington, politicians blasted the decision and crowded the Capitol steps to recite the Pledge en masse. Under then attorney general John Ashcroft, the Justice Department appealed the Ninth Circuit decision, joining the school district being sued by Newdow. In October 2003, the U.S. Supreme Court agreed to hear an appeal. Oral arguments were set for March 2004. (There is more about the hearing and its outcome in Chapter 9.)

As the pending Supreme Court case drew more and more attention to the "under God" controversy, I received a phone call from my niece Arianna. A sophomore in high school at the time, Arianna was doing a paper on the issue, and my brother had urged her to call me for guidance. As it turned out, I was the beneficiary of my niece's clear thinking.

Arianna began telling me about her research in the diffident way school kids broach their ideas with adults. As she talked, though, it became clear that she had learned a great deal about the history of the Pledge and had thought hard about the "under God" debate. "The theme of my paper," she said, "is how ironic it is that the Pledge of Allegiance was written as something to bring people together and now it is pulling people apart." Ironic indeed.

The "under God" quarrel reveals the double-edged power of the Pledge. As a ritual nearly universal in American life, reciting the Pledge is really the closest thing we have to a national prayer. In this respect, though, the Pledge taps into a deep-rooted tension in American society between the religious and the secular, and it draws out the white-hot emotions that this interplay can produce.

The Pledge reveals a deep division over how best to express love of country and its founding principles. To some, the Pledge is a sublime ode to essential American ideals. To others, it is a hypocritical profession of standards—"liberty and justice for all"—that the nation fails to meet. To some, the Pledge is an opportunity to profess patriotic sentiment. For others it is a noxious test of patriotism, a loyalty oath.

The way we think and talk about the Pledge can cast light on the political and philosophical arguments that animate and divide Americans today. A retired high-school English teacher named Jim Kraus told me that, in his classroom days, he had recited the Pledge with his students, or not, depending on his feelings about the political situation at the moment. Jim's approach to the Pledge is, I think, a striking example of a general phenomenon. People's attitudes toward the Pledge often parallel their basic beliefs and feelings about the country.

There are parallels also between the history of the Pledge and the changing state of the nation. Over the 118 years since Bellamy wrote down the original version of the Pledge, the vicissitudes of the flag salute have vividly reflected the state of the nation and the popular mood—born, as it was, at a time when anxieties over the impact of mass immigration coexisted with expansive optimism about the nation's future. The Pledge was the focus of intensive use during the First and Second World Wars, during the Cold War, and during the Vietnam War, and it was a fulcrum of controversy during each of those periods, as it has been in our own era of uncertainty and perceived peril.

What exactly does the Pledge mean? There is no single answer. Francis Bellamy left several accounts of what he had in mind when he composed the text. Since then, though, the Pledge has developed multiple levels and dimensions of meaning. Today, no two Americans are likely to agree on every facet of its significance. Inevitably, though, when I talk to people about the Pledge of Allegiance, the conversation always comes around to what they see as the nation's essential values. So it seems to have been from the beginning. Francis Bellamy's brief salute to the flag has had an almost magical power to galvanize people's deepest feelings and beliefs about who we are and ought to be as a nation. In that sense, the story of the Pledge of Allegiance is the story of America and the American people.

2. THE ERA OF THE PLEDGE

The Pledge of Allegiance was a product of its time, a time that was in many ways like the present. The nation was haunted by war—a bitter and bloody Civil War that had ended twenty-five years earlier yet was still very much alive in the national consciousness. As in contemporary America, technological innovation was reshaping the economy, and working people were scrambling to adapt. Then as now, the chief executives of the dominant companies and the financiers who managed the flow of capital had amassed staggering fortunes, and the country's private wealth lay mostly in the coffers of a super-rich elite, while an undereducated, underprivileged underclass languished in urban slums.

As in America today, waves of immigrants were helping to meet the country's manpower needs—some of them fleeing conditions so wretched that they were happy to do the menial jobs American workers shunned. The country fretted about the impact these foreign-born masses would have on society, and there was much argument in Washington, in the communications media, and around the cracker barrel over what measures would be appropriate to control the influx.

At the ebb of the nineteenth century, as at the rise of the twenty-first, changes in the economy, changes in the makeup of the population, and a growing fear that the nation's fundamental identity was in jeopardy had led to a surge in patriotic activities and public displays of patriotism.

For all its similarities to the present, however, the era when the Pledge of Allegiance came to life was a unique and pivotal moment in the life of the nation. In 1892, the year Francis Bellamy set the original words of the Pledge on paper, America was a brawny adolescent striding out of its frontier past toward a new era. In fact, in 1890, the U.S. Census Bureau had officially declared the frontier closed; the land of opportunity was now metropolitan, and people were streaming to American cities from farms and villages around the country and across the seas.

The country had grown from what had been a second-rank economic presence in 1865 to a full-fledged industrial powerhouse. By 1890, the value of goods manufactured in the United States nearly equaled that of England, France, and Germany combined. In 1892, the output of Carnegie Steel alone was more than half the total product of all the steel companies in Great Britain. Within the decade, the United States would begin to flex its muscles in the geopolitical arena with military adventures in Cuba and the Philippines that would prove to be the coup de grâce of the four-hundred-year-old Spanish empire.

As the nation hurtled toward the twentieth century, and the wonders and the horrors that awaited it, the legacies of the waning era still lived on in the national psyche—none more vividly than the Civil War. The treaty at Appomattox, twenty-five years before, still seemed recent to many, and the trauma of the conflict was in no way forgotten. Of a national population totaling thirty-four million when the shooting began, nearly four million men had served in the Union and Confederate armies. One in four of the combatants had died or was wounded. Everyone Francis Bellamy's age or older remembered men marching off to war from their towns and cities never to return, or hobbling home on one leg and a crutch. The postwar Reconstruction was conceived in idealism, but despite some real accomplishments, rather than salve the internecine wounds it only rubbed them raw again. For many Americans in the 1890s, the country was still divided between Union blue and Confederate gray. And when Bellamy was planning the grand nationwide Public Schools Celebration, he took pains to ask congressional leaders for their opinions about including veterans groups from the north and south, for fear of reigniting sectional passions.

Along with the enduring pain of national schism and human loss, the postwar era brought fresh blows to the American self-concept. Lincoln had been assassinated, Andrew Johnson impeached, and the Union hero turned president Ulysses S. Grant had turned out to be a hapless dupe for fleecers and flimflammers. Meanwhile, civil rights advances achieved under Reconstruction were nullified during Grant's watch by a rash of new white supremacy laws. Then there came economic recession (the Panic of 1873), and before long another assassination (Garfield, shot in the back on July 2, 1881).

It is remarkable, then, to read what Bernard A. Weisberger would later write about the America of 1890 for the *Life History of the United States:*

> The average citizen believed that his social order was the world's best and his political system the world's wisest. . . . The future would be ever richer, more spacious for each new generation.

To the extent that Weisberger's description of the national mood at the time is accurate (more about that shortly), it may reflect in part a popular infatuation with the mystique of industrialization that was sweeping the Western world. The miracles of technology and their promise of a brave new world ahead were celebrated at world's fairs in London (1851), Philadelphia (1876), Paris (1889), Chicago (1893), and, again in Paris (1900), with the Eiffel Tower the most spectacular and enduring product of the period. Hand in hand with late-nineteenth-century technophilia was the return to prominence of that ancient object of mania: money.

Not that wealth had come into the hands of the many. In fact, the final decade of the nineteenth century was an era of huge income inequality between the very richest and the rest of the population—much like the first decade of the twenty-first century. In 1890, the wealthiest one percent of the population received the same total income as the bottom half and owned more property than the other 99 percent. (As for the present-day wealth gap, according to a 2006 report from the Federal Reserve, the top 10 percent of income earners in the United States possessed 70 percent of the wealth, and the richest 5 percent owned more than the bottom 95 percent.)

Even though riches eluded the great majority of Americans in the 1890s—as now—the fortunes created by the spectacular industrial expansion inflamed the popular imagination. Those who had cashed in were flaunting their new wealth in gaudy displays—which the contemporary observer Thorstein Veblen described as "conspicuous consumption"—and the man in the street found it mesmerizing. Money and the making of it had become a national obsession; at least it seemed that way to Mark Twain, who dubbed the era the Gilded Age in his novel of the same name (coauthored with his Hartford, Connecticut, neighbor Charles Dudley Warner). Patrician statesmen like Henry Adams were being replaced as the most admired Americans by hard-driving industrialists like Andrew Carnegie, John D. Rockefeller, and Cornelius Vanderbilt, and by financiers like J. P. Morgan, who had amassed their riches thanks in part to the lack of an income tax (which didn't come into effect until 1913) and the absence of antitrust laws (the first of which was enacted in 1890).

Not everyone agreed with the cutthroat rapaciousness of the money moguls, but many couldn't help wanting their own share of the loot. What's more, like the day traders riding the tech-stock bubble of the 1990s, the unschooled speculators of the Gilded Era marveled at their own apparent canniness: "I wasn't worth a cent two years ago, and now I owe two millions of dollars," gushes one of Twain and Warner's characters.

Of course, for all the glittering fantasies of striking it rich, most Americans merely toiled away as cogs in the great economic machine that was generating the fortunes of the well-off. The era of American rugged individualism when most people made a living on their own as farmers or craftsmen or tradesmen was giving way: America was becoming a nation of industrial laborers and office workers on someone else's payroll.

Meanwhile, with government assistance to the poor virtually nonexistent, those who fell through the cracks of the industrial revolution landed hard. Guests at the Vanderbilts' Fifth Avenue mansion in New York City dined off golden plates, but fifty blocks south, on the Lower East Side of Manhattan, the poor lived in Dickensian squalor. Families crammed into windowless rooms, street urchins played in trash-filled alleys, and homeless men sprawled head to toe on bare wood planks in primitive lodging houses. It is a fair guess that the vision of an ever-richer future was lost on the members of this rapidly growing underclass. To the general public, bedazzled by the posturing of the rich and the nouveaux riches, the poor had remained conveniently invisible. Then a reporter named Jacob Riis wrote about them in newspaper articles and in a book, *How the Other Half Lives,* published in 1890. Riis, a Danish immigrant who had experienced poverty firsthand, backed up his writing with stark photographs that shocked readers: haggard men staring from the floor of a flop house, and smudge-faced toddlers in a tenement kitchen wide-eyed in the glare of Riis's flash-powder illumination. Other writers and social critics described the plight of women and children working backbreaking shifts under deplorable conditions in factories and sweatshops.

To explain the gap between the opulence of the rich and the misery that the work of Riis and others revealed, self-made magnates like Andrew Carnegie embraced a convenient idea:

"survival of the fittest," the catchphrase of a philosophy that came to be known as "social Darwinism." Before Charles Darwin ever used the saying, it was made famous by the British social philosopher Herbert Spencer. Spencer advanced a worldview in which everything under the sun would continually get better and better, if only humankind would avoid interfering with nature's inexorable progression toward perfection. When Darwin published his world-shaking *Origin of Species,* in 1859, Spencer pounced on the idea of "natural selection" and extended it to the realm of human interaction and commerce. (Darwin eventually picked up Spencer's "survival of the fittest" epithet and used it in his own writings.) Spencer asserted that governments should stay away from any kind of business regulation. A laissez-faire approach would ensure optimal economic development—the strongest businesses would thrive and those that couldn't keep up would be swept aside.

This way of thinking was tailor-made for men like Carnegie and John D. Rockefeller, eager to reconcile their ruthlessly monopolistic business practices and, in Carnegie's case, brutal treatment of workers with their self-image as God-fearing Christians. "We accept and welcome . . . the concentration of business, industrial and commercial, in the hands of a few," Carnegie said, "as being not only beneficial but essential to the future progress of the race."

Some pushed the eugenic interpretation of the gap between the haves and the have-nots a step further. S.C.T. Dodd, the vaunted general counsel for Rockefeller's Standard Oil Company, asserted that poverty exists "because the nature of the devil has made some men weak and imbecile and others lazy and worthless, and neither man nor God can do much for one who will do nothing for himself."

In the face of such smug sophistry, Americans in need of a moral compass to help guide them might find that even their church had been co-opted. Protestantism was America's religion at the time—two out of three churchgoers identified with one of the many Protestant denominations. As part of the Establishment, much of the mainstream Protestant church found itself in sync with business. According to historian Sidney Fine:

> Nowhere . . . did the business spirit find greater favor than in the Protestant church. . . . Wealthy business figures were appointed to church boards in increasing numbers, and men of business ability were in demand to serve as church officials. Even the Baptists, who had prided themselves on being a poor man's denomination, ceased to express contempt for wealth. . . .

However, strong voices would emerge within the church and the churchgoing laity, who resisted the sweep of materialist values and the self-justifying rationales of the well-healed. Protestant clergymen Washington Gladden and Walter Rauschenbusch were among the most renowned critics of Gilded Age materialism at the time. They denounced the corrosive impact on society of the cartels like Standard Oil and the men behind them. Of Rockefeller, Gladden would write in 1905:

> [Rockefeller] is the representative of a great system that has become a public enemy. The organization which he represents has been and is now a gigantic oppressor of the people. . . . [It is] abundantly clear that this great fortune has been built up by the transgression and the evasion of law and by methods which are at war with the first principles of morality. Are we, as Christians, forbidden to judge this sort of thing? I rather think it is our business to be swift witnesses against it.

Gladden, a Congregational minister, wrote influentially and entered politics in an effort to push reforms, serving for two years on the city council of Columbus, Ohio. Rauschenbusch, a Baptist, was a pastor in the Hell's Kitchen area of New York City and a religious educator. They and others advanced an activist religious practice known as the Social Gospel, which called on believers to assert Christian principles in the here and now to support economic and social justice. Meanwhile, the needs of the poor and socially deprived inspired the founding of urban settlement houses, like Jane Addams's Hull House in Chicago, the Neighborhood Guild in New York, and Andover House in Boston, which brought some social services, education, and recreation to city slums.

Representing the interests of wage earners, the American labor movement began to coalesce as a force to contend with. By 1886, the broad-based Knights of Labor counted as members more than 700,000 skilled and unskilled workers. The movement progressed in fits and starts over ensuing decades of tumult and periodic crisis.

In a more visionary realm, writer-philosopher Edward Bellamy, Francis' first cousin, imagined a society based on equitable distribution of resources. His best-selling 1888 novel, *Looking Backward*, tells a kind of Rip van Winkle story in which a man wakes up, in the year 2000, after a century of sleep to discover a world founded on mutual cooperation and concern, rather than competition. He finds a country that has been cleansed of its nineteenth-century flaws and transformed into a peaceful and thoughtful society free of unemployment, starvation, or poverty, and the state is the only employer. The change occurred gradually, without violence. A beneficent government controls capital and apportions the gross national product equally among all. Bellamy's dream of institutionalized equity and brotherly love attracted a following of intellectuals and idealists who embraced the tenets of what came to be known alternately as Nationalism and Christian socialism. Among those active in promoting these ideas in speeches and published essays was Edward's younger cousin, the future author of the Pledge of Allegiance, Reverend Francis Bellamy. (As we will see later, Francis, a fervent idealist, also shared some of the era's crass prejudices.)

The single most far-reaching phenomenon of the era when the Pledge came into being was immigration. In 1892, the year the Pledge came to be, Ellis Island opened in New York Harbor as a processing center for people arriving by ship from Europe in ever-increasing numbers. The former naval munitions depot was converted at a cost of $500,000 to replace a smaller reception area in Castle Garden, a onetime fortification and amusement center in Battery Park at the southern tip of Manhattan. That facility had been overwhelmed. Between 1881 and 1890, the number of foreign-born people entering the United States had almost doubled compared to the previous decade—from 2.8 million to 5.2 million. (The aggregate foreign-born population in 1890 was more than 9 million, almost 15 percent of the national total, the biggest proportion ever. By comparison, in 2000, the Census Bureau counted 28.4 million people living in the United States who were born abroad, at 10 percent the highest proportion since 1930.)

Immigrants played a crucial role in the economy by helping to fill an ongoing need for manual labor. In 1890, 56 percent of the labor force in manufacturing and mechanical industries was foreign born or of foreign parentage. But then as now, the increasing influx of immigrants raised fears and bared some ugly prejudices. Would the new arrivals take jobs, use up public resources, cause an increase in crime? Would their language, their customs, their differentness overwhelm the nation's dominant Anglo-Saxon culture?

America's traditional image as a nation of immigrants and a refuge for the downtrodden is well earned. The timeline of immigration to America in colonial times is famously marked with the arrivals of people fleeing intolerance and persecution—from the Puritans in 1620, to Lord Baltimore's Catholics in 1634, to the first Jewish immigrants fleeing maltreatment in Brazil (1654), to the Quakers (1681), the Mennonites (1688), and the Huguenots (1685). And yet, almost from the beginning, Americans have exhibited mixed feelings toward those who came after them. In the late 1600s, popular prejudice drew official support when some colonial governments passed measures discriminating against Catholics and the Scotch-Irish (who originally had been brought into the colonies as servants):

> "The common fear," a Pennsylvania official explained, "is that if they [the Scotch-Irish] thus continue to come they will make themselves proprietors of the Province."

In the early days of independence from Britain, the young United States of America had virtually no legal or bureaucratic barriers to immigration. (One reason for welcoming all was the practical fact that there were huge territories to settle and defend. The first federal census, in 1790, counted a total population in the young nation of only 3.2 million occupying more than 700,000 square miles of territory.) In 1793, President George Washington enunciated an "open-door policy" that resounded with the democratic idealism that Americans like to think of as a defining national characteristic: "The bosom of America is open to receive not only the opulent and respectable stranger, but the oppressed and persecuted of all nations and religions; whom we shall welcome to a participation of all our rights and privileges."

By 1798, however, Congress had voted into law the oxymoronically titled Alien Friends Act, which empowered the president to deport any noncitizen who might be "dangerous to the peace and safety of the United States." This was soon followed by the Naturalization Act, which established a hefty residency requirement of fourteen years for an immigrant to be eligible for citizenship. In 1801, though, after a power shift in Congress, the Alien Friends Act was allowed to lapse and the residency requirement for naturalization was shortened to five years.

The first enduring restriction on immigration came in 1882, when Congress passed the Chinese Exclusion Act, spurred by lobbying from Western states, where Chinese immigrants had helped build railroads and mine the gold and silver fields. The law barred Chinese from entering the country for ten years (except for students, merchants, and children of Chinese-American citizens). Rather than only a decade, the prohibition on Chinese immigration stayed in effect until 1943.

Although the Chinese Exclusion Act was the only time in American history that an ethnic group or nationality was singled out to be prohibited from immigration, it was of course neither the first nor the last time that a minority was the target of open bigotry and hostility. For millions who have come to this country over the years and who are still arriving from around the world, the mystique of America as a land of opportunity and safe haven has been very much a reality. Unfortunately, though, along with the Scotch-Irish, the Germans, and the Chinese, successions of immigrant groups have experienced discrimination and violence in their adopted homeland.

Twenty-five years before signing the Declaration of Independence, no less a figure than Benjamin Franklin expressed unblushing antipathy toward German newcomers in Pennsylvania. In a 1751 screed, he wrote about immigrants from the German Palatinate:

> Why should the Palatine Boors be suffered to swarm
> into our Settlements, and by herding together, estab-
> lish their Language and Manners, to the Exclusion
> of ours? Why should Pennsylvania, founded by the

English, become a Colony of Aliens, who will shortly
be so numerous as to Germanize us instead of our
Anglifying them . . . ?

This passage from a revered founding father is an early example
of a mind-set that decades later came to be known as "nativism"—
virulent opposition to supposedly inferior groups seen as a threat
to the predominant culture. In his attack, the word-savvy Mr.
Franklin used terms like "swarm" and "herding" to dehumanize
the people who were the object of derision, an approach that
would be typical of later nativist diatribes.

In the great wave of immigration to America during the
1830s and 1840s, the Irish outnumbered all other nationalities.
Escaping famine and oppression in their own country, many
found themselves crowded into disease-rife slums on this side
of the Atlantic and shut out of the jobs that might lift them out
of poverty. (The now infamous phrase "No Irish Need Apply"
was familiar in employment postings and rental ads.) Portrayed as ignorant, dirty, and immoral, the Irish were, worst of
all to their detractors, Catholic. Many Americans saw Catholics as a subversive group controlled by the pope in Rome and
a threat to the governing principles of the primordially Protestant nation.

Anti-Catholicism and other nativist sentiments entered mainstream politics with the rise in the 1850s of the Know-Nothing
Party. Officially called at various times the American Party or
the Native American Party, the group had nothing to do with
indigenous peoples and everything to do with playing on fear
and prejudice for political advantage. (Originally a quasi-secret
organization with hokey recognition signals, the party earned its
nickname because its members, when asked about the organization, supposedly replied, "I know nothing.") With anti-Catholic,
anti-Irish tenets as their chief focus, the Know Nothings gained
control of several state governments, mostly in the Northeast,

and sent more than a few representatives to the U.S. Congress. The party pushed for laws limiting immigration and tightening naturalization requirements, while Know Nothing legislators set up committees to investigate alleged malfeasance in Catholic institutions. In the presidential election of 1856, former president Millard Fillmore represented the Know Nothings as a third-party candidate. Almost 900,000 Americans cast ballots for him (more than one in five voters) and he won the state of Maryland.

While its electoral successes lent the Know Nothings a veneer of legitimacy, the party attracted a thug element that favored intimidation and violence over electioneering. In 1844, nativist precursors of the Know Nothings sparked anti–Irish Catholic riots in Philadelphia that resulted in more than twenty deaths. Ten years later, in Baltimore, a gang of Know-Nothing boosters called the Plug Uglies attacked polling places on election day. Writing in 1998 in the Baltimore *City Paper*, Brennen Jensen described their approach:

> Their methods were crude but effective. While today we vote in secrecy, voters of that era brought their marked ballots to the polls with them. Know Nothing ballots were gaudily striped and easy to spot. When a voter approached carrying Know Nothing colors, he was greeted with backslaps and smiles. When a rival ballot was spied, thugs chanted "Meet him on the ice!" and pounced like feral dogs. Fists, paving stones, and knives were part of the arsenal, but the favorite weapon was the easy-to-conceal awl. Shoemakers used these pointed tools to punch holes in leather; the Know Nothings used them to punch holes in their rivals.

On election day 1854, the Plug Uglies triggered riots in Baltimore that left eight dead. In Louisville, Kentucky, election day

1855 became known as "Bloody Monday" after Know-Nothing mobs attacked Germans and Irish voters, leaving twenty-two dead and a trail of arson and looting.

Although the Know-Nothing Party fizzled soon after the 1856 elections, hostility toward immigrants and spates of nativist violence recurred in America through the rest of the nineteenth century and beyond. Favorite targets in the West were the Chinese, more than 200,000 of whom had crossed the Pacific between 1850 and 1880, before the Exclusion Act. As with the Irish-Catholics and German immigrants, the Chinese were resented as competitors for jobs, housing, and other resources in California, Colorado, and other areas of the West where they had settled. The Chinese were also feared and loathed because of their otherness. Officially sanctioning popular sentiments, state legislation banned them from mining jobs, barred them from public schools, and even prohibited them from testifying in court against whites.

Once a group is officially depersonalized and painted as a menace, grassroots violence often follows. In 1871 a mob attacked Chinatown in Los Angeles, burning and looting homes and businesses and killing some twenty Chinese men and boys. Other violence against Chinese in California followed, especially as economic conditions deteriorated nationwide and jobs became scarce after the Panic of 1873. In 1876, a group of angry citizens who counted themselves as members of the nativist Order of Caucasians attacked Chinese woodcutters in Truckee, California, setting their cabin afire as they slept and firing on them when they ran outside to fight the blaze. In 1885, at a Rock Springs, Wyoming, coal mine, a group of striking union miners of Welsh and Swedish descent attacked and burned the homes of Chinese miners who had been brought in as replacement workers, killing twenty-eight. Such attacks on Chinese seldom led to successful prosecutions, even when it was well known who the perpetrators were. Chinese witnesses, of course, weren't allowed to give evidence in court.

As new waves of immigrants crossed the Atlantic during the 1880s and 1890s, xenophobic reactions and episodes of violence against ethnic minorities increased elsewhere in the country as well. The issue for those on the attack wasn't simply the volume of new arrivals, but who the latest newcomers were and where they came from. The traditional view of the prototypical American at the time was someone of northern and western European descent, reflecting the origins of the large majority of immigrants up until the 1880s. But in the last decades of the nineteenth century and the first part of the twentieth century, the numbers coming from southern and eastern Europe mushroomed, spurred by poverty, privation, persecution, and other political, economic, and social conditions. In the same period, the totals from Ireland, Germany, and Great Britain trailed off dramatically. Of the 3.22 million people who came to the United States during the 1890s, more than half were from Italy and eastern Europe. If the Irish felt unwelcome when their influx peaked during the 1840s and 1850s, well, at least they typically were fair-skinned and spoke English. On the other hand, the Italians, the Jews from Russia, the Slavs, Magyars, Greeks, Portuguese, and other groups whose immigration tallies increased during the period were considered by many Americans of more traditional ethnic extraction to be beyond the pale—fundamentally different and occupying a lower niche on the scale of human development.

These attitudes were widely held, openly expressed in educated, respectable circles, and given currency by individuals considered part of the intelligentsia. Francis Amasa Walker, a renowned economist at the time, portrayed the new strain of immigrants as "beaten men from beaten races, representing the worst failures in the struggle of existence." A group of young Harvard graduates founded the Immigration Restriction League, which zealously lobbied Congress to regulate immigration based on ethnic origin and to institute literacy tests for immigrants. In 1896, Congress passed such a bill, sponsored by the powerful Massachusetts congressman (later senator) Henry Cabot Lodge (who, in the next chapter, will play a walk-on role in the story of the Pledge). President Grover Cleveland denounced ethnic quotas and literacy tests as contrary to the American spirit and vetoed the measure. Similar legislation, passed and vetoed by successive presidents, finally took effect in 1917, after Congress overrode President Woodrow Wilson's veto.

The changing face of immigration, and the threat it seemed to imply to a traditional view of American identity, was one of the factors behind another, more benign phenomenon: a mushrooming growth in the number of patriotic organizations and a notable increase in public displays of national pride. The 1890s saw the birth of groups like the Daughters of the American Revolution (DAR), the Sons of the American Revolution (SAR), and other hereditary associations that sought to identify themselves with the heroic origins of American nationhood.

Beyond confirming that the forbearers of its members were longtime residents of the New World, these organizations saw fervent patriotism as a central part of their franchise. While the motivation for joining the groups was in part snobbery and in part a simple urge toward social affiliation, there was in the impulses behind their formation an implied circling of the wagons. In his book *Patriotism on Parade,* Wallace Evans Davies offers this observation:

> What was happening was that an industrialized urbanized society was dissolving the standards, mores, and bonds of a simpler rural order and instead was producing a land more and more diversified in national origin, religion, and cultural inheritance, with no national church or royal family or other cohesive traditions and symbols, perhaps in the near future not

even a common language, some feared. Consequently many turned to patriotism as a sort of secular religion to unite the American republic.

However much defensiveness may have motivated the surge in patriotism, there was a genuinely American exuberance to it as well. In his book *Flag: An American Biography,* Marc Leepson describes the growing popularity in those days of displaying and venerating the Stars and Stripes:

> Flags flew from public and private buildings, ceremonies took place at city halls and other municipal venues, streetcars in big cities were decked out with flags and bunting, and flag commemorations took place in public schools.

In terms of size, a scheme for the grandest flag began to take shape in 1890 when William O. McDowell, a zealous and imaginative booster of all things patriotic, launched a campaign to get a gigantic flagpole constructed on the Navesink Highlands in New Jersey so that ship passengers bound for New York Harbor would see the American standard as they caught sight of shore. McDowell, a prominent Garden State financier, was instrumental in founding both the Sons and the Daughters of the American Revolution, the two most prominent heredity groups commemorating American patriots. Membership in both organizations required proof of being a direct descendant of someone who had aided in the independence effort. While some DAR chapters dated to 1890, Congress gave the group an official charter in 1896; SAR, begun by McDowell in New York City's Fraunces Tavern in 1889 (the centennial of George Washington's inauguration), received its congressional charter in 1906, signed by President Theodore Roosevelt, who was also a member.

In 1891 the U.S. commissioner of education, William T.

Harris, appointed to his post by President Benjamin Harrison in 1889, approved a proposal to fly flags over every public school building in the country, thus reflecting what author Wallace Evans Davies described as "a curious faith in the beneficial effect that the mere physical presence of the banner had upon youth."

Soon there would come an opportunity to focus national pride on a national scale. With the approach of the four hundredth anniversary of Columbus's voyage of discovery to America, the U.S. Congress authorized funds for a new world's fair in Chicago. A major thrust of this "Columbian" Exposition would be to celebrate the United States as the full florescence of civilization in the New World. Groundbreaking for the Chicago expo was scheduled for October 1892, which set in motion a chain of events that would lead to the birth of the Pledge of Allegiance.

3. HOW IT HAPPENED

History, a teacher once told me, is a conjunction of institutions and ideas, individuals and events. In the case of the Pledge of Allegiance, the confluence seems almost magical—people and forces coming together at exactly the right moment to give life to something brand new.

The story begins with a long-lived periodical called the *Youth's Companion*. Published in Boston, the *Companion* was born in 1827 as an offshoot for young readers of a religiously oriented digest. The *Companion* developed into one of the leading periodicals of its day, offering children in the preelectronic era a window on the world beyond the garden gate.

One reader, looking back on her mid-nineteenth-century girlhood in a small country town near Worcester, Massachusetts, recalled the excitement she felt awaiting her weekly copy of the *Companion*. Mary Davis and her sister had scrounged rags and collected chestnuts to raise the one-dollar cost of a subscription. The magazine reached them via the weekly market wagon: "With what eagerness did we often watch the slow approach over distant hills of that white-topped wagon, and on its arrival how carefully would we scan its contents till we discovered the much-desired paper!"

The rise of the *Companion* began in 1867 when it came under the control of an enterprising and creative businessman named Daniel Sharp Ford. Applying astute editorial instincts and innovative business practices, he transformed a pious provincial children's digest into a national publication. From a circulation of forty-eight hundred when Ford took over, the *Companion*'s distribution had grown to nearly half a million by 1892—at the time one of the largest of any American magazine. (For reasons obscure, Ford named the umbrella organization that published the *Companion* the Perry Mason Company. The writer Erle Stanley Gardner later said that when he used the name for the protagonist of his popular courtroom book series, he probably subconsciously remembered it from his boyhood reading of the *Companion*.)

Daniel Ford retooled *Youth's Companion* as a family magazine with appeal to adults as well as children. He attracted name writers like Harriet Beecher Stowe, Emily Dickinson, William James, and Mark Twain. Besides enriching the content, Ford used pioneering techniques to attract advertisers to its pages and he set up aggressive marketing and promotion programs. One of his most effective tactics was the use of premiums—products, cash bonuses, and other inducements to acquire subscribers—a harbinger of the toy in the Happy Meal today, or the million-dollar sweepstake offers from magazine publishers, or the bonus cell-phone minutes for referring another customer. For the *Youth's Companion*, premiums proved a big success—stimulating subscriptions and generating new revenue streams beyond advertising and circulation.

At a time when delivering marketing messages in anything larger than tiny agate type was looked upon by traditionalists as unseemly, the *Companion* splashed its premium promotions across the page in big bold type. One ad promised readers who sold subscriptions to friends and relatives **"An Equal Division of FIVE THOUSAND DOLLARS IN CASH."** Readers who reached the sales quota could also choose from a profusion of merchandise—from watches to fountain pens to moonstone rings. (The practice of tapping existing customers to get new ones—the "friend get a friend" approach—is one of Ford's techniques still favored by magazine publishers and other direct marketers.)

Through the *Companion*, premium items were also available for direct purchase. The magazine published an annual catalog issue offering products of an abundance and variety that Amazon .com might be proud to offer today—laying hens and singing canaries, watch fobs and steam engines, bedsteads and jackknives, and on and on.

Of all the premiums the *Companion* offered, one stands out above all others: the American flag. Premium campaigns around the flag proved immensely successful for the magazine, in both financial and promotional terms. At the same time, the *Companion*'s efforts had a lasting impact on the place of the American flag in the life of the nation.

Today, public schools and flags go together like french fries and ketchup. Travel around any town or city in the United States and you can count on seeing the Stars and Stripes in front of, or atop, most public schools (and in many classrooms as well). It wasn't always so. If any one person deserves credit for establishing this ubiquitous practice, it is James B. Upham.

Upham joined *Youth's Companion* in 1886. A nephew by marriage to Daniel Ford, he signed on to lead a new department, one dedicated to developing the potential of premiums. Upham combined patriotic zeal with a genius for promotion—and he showed no hesitation in using the one in service of the other. There was nothing cynical, though, about Upham's patriotism. A staunch New Englander, Upham as a schoolboy heard classroom declamations every Friday of Daniel Webster's orations on the birth of the union. "We were brought up on the air of patriotism," he recalled. As an adult, Upham was distressed to perceive that appreciation for the blessings of American democracy had gone into decline—taking a backseat in the Gilded Age to pursuit of the almighty dollar. He worried that a fading of patriotic awareness could lead to a citizenry that did not know enough nor care enough to defend democracy against erosion from within or attack from outside.

The arrival in New York Harbor and other American

seaports of shipload after shipload of immigrants made the challenge all the more acute. To invigorate the national spirit and to advance civic consciousness, Upham believed in a need to instill patriotism at a popular level, especially among young citizens of the future. His uncle concurred.

Ford and Upham saw promoting national pride as part of the *Companion*'s mission—this at a time when the idea of "mission" in a business context was more than a pro forma statement of goals and principles. Like a substantial segment of educated churchgoers in late-nineteenth-century America, they embraced an activist view of religion along the lines of the "Social Gospel" approach that a few years later would come to be identified with Walter Rauschenbusch.

They took a similar view of their duties as citizens. They felt obligated to further the essential moral values and the philosophical principles they believed in. For Ford and Upham, these included the liberties and the egalitarian ideals they saw as the bedrock of American democracy. If this evangelizing complemented the periodical's editorial franchise and helped increase profits, so much the better.

After a few months at the helm of the Premiums Department, Upham began to think about premium offerings that might support the *Companion*'s patriotic mission while also serving its commercial imperative. His thoughts turned to the American flag. What more readily identifiable symbol of the United States and its principles could there be? The red, white, and blue offered visual shorthand for a nation's values that even the youngest schoolchildren could relate to.

Although patriotic activities and displays were on the increase at the time, the flag was not yet the ubiquitous fixture at schools and other public buildings that it is today. To reach the young, Upham decided, every public school should have a flag. Focusing on public schools would highlight their importance to society as crucibles of citizenship—a conviction not shared by a significant bloc of citizens who opposed using taxes to finance government-sponsored education. Spotlighting public schools would also help counter what Ford and Upham saw as a disproportionate influence of church-sponsored education. Both were active churchgoers but they were philosophically opposed to an education system under the aegis of religion, which they feared was a threat to the separation of church and state. (Upham was a Mason, a group known at the time to oppose the influence of the Roman Catholic Church in particular.)

Upham launched a campaign in the *Companion* of advertisements and supporting editorial material urging young readers to sell certificates to family, friends, and neighbors at ten cents apiece until they saved up the ten dollars needed to purchase a school flag from the *Companion*. The Flag Over the Schoolhouse program, as it came to be known, was a triumph by every measure. Beginning in 1888, the *Companion* sold increasing numbers of flags each year, peaking at more than twenty-five thousand in 1891. While helping launch a national tradition of displaying flags at schools, Upham's venture also scored a trifecta for the magazine—raising patriotic awareness, achieving valuable promotion, and generating income from the sale of flags.

Besides standards for schools, the *Companion*'s premium operation sold many other kinds of flags and flag paraphernalia: a pocket flag with carrying case, wall flags for the home, flag mending kits, and more. (Later, again combining ideology with self-interest, the *Companion* supported state laws requiring public schools to fly the flag, which many states adopted.) Upham also ran a parallel flag promotion: an essay contest on "The Patriotic Influence of the American Flag When Raised over the Public Schools." The school with the best essay in each state received a flag measuring nine by fifteen feet.

To further nurture the spirit of patriotism, in 1891 the *Companion* announced the founding of the Lyceum League of America—a network of local youth groups whose mission was to celebrate the value of American citizenship through lectures, debates, and other activities. Within a year, the *Companion*'s Lyceum League numbered twelve hundred societies with thirty thousand members. (Upham modeled these societies on New England village lyceums, which had bloomed earlier in the nineteenth century. Offering speakers and cultural programs, these groups were often a community's sole source of culture and entertainment.)

As the school flag campaign rolled forward, Upham set his imagination in gear for a new inspiration. It came to him in the summer of 1891 while vacationing in his native New Hampshire. As he reclined in the shade of a pine tree, savoring the aromas of boughs and bark and sap, his mind drifted toward the upcoming World Columbian Exposition. The official groundbreaking for the Chicago world's fair was set to take place amid great fanfare in October 1892. Why couldn't the *Companion* hitch its wagon to this very powerful horse?

When he returned to the office, Upham began to flesh out his idea. And it wasn't long before he found the perfect connection: Columbus Day. There was as yet no national holiday celebrating the discovery of America, but many localities, New York City prominent among them, sponsored big celebrations.

In fact, Columbus Day fests in some American towns dated back to 1792, the three hundredth anniversary of the Italian explorer's grand transatlantic voyage. Italian-Americans, particularly in New York, began routinely commemorating Columbus Day as an expression of pride in their Italian heritage. These early tributes were also linked to a desire among many Catholics to establish a rightful place as Americans when Catholicism was widely viewed with considerable scorn. These Columbus commemorations were not the type of public expression we associate with a modern holiday—parades and speeches—but were instead considered an opportunity to visit one's church, to acknowledge the day in prayer. And they served to remind other Americans of the ethnic and religious background of what most people at the time considered to be the *first* American.

The number of Catholic Americans had been instantly amplified with the Louisiana Purchase in 1803. And despite ongoing suspicion of them by Protestants, by 1850 Catholics had become the largest religious denomination in the United States. Their numbers grew even more rapidly with the immigrant surge that began in the 1870s and continued into the early twentieth century, when Catholics would represent one-sixth of the population. Between 1880 and 1890, the number of Italian immigrants alone jumped from less than one percent of total immigrants to over 2 percent; by 1900, Italians represented nearly 5 percent of the ten million people who entered the country that year—almost all of them Catholic.

Despite growing numbers, their status as second-class citizens—by virtue of their assumed loyalties to spiritual Rome rather than secular Washington—was certainly on the minds of the creators of what would become the largest Catholic fraternal organization in the United States, the Knights of Columbus. Founded in 1882, the Knights were early supporters of Columbus Day celebrations at the local level, and the growing population of Italian-American immigrants, most of whom were Catholic, gave the organization increasing political clout. Thus the Knights of Columbus's support for a nationwide quadricentennial observation of Columbus Day was not just an important part of what would become a groundswell of enthusiasm for Upham's idea, but also a way of demonstrating Catholic loyalty to America.

The second part of Upham's plan—to make public schools the center of the quadricentennial event—was equally well-timed, as the country was just emerging from a long and hard debate about the value of public education to the young nation, with the proponents, like W. T. Harris and Benjamin Harrison, winning the day and leading to the establishment of free public schools for everyone. "The public school is exactly the right institution to take charge of this celebration," Chicago congressman Allan Durborow would tell Francis Bellamy. "There is a direct line of connection between the determination of Columbus to break through the limitations of the Middle Ages and the educational system which represents the modern spirit of enlightenment."

Finally, unlike other commemorations, which honored individuals at their births or deaths, Upham could choose an October 12 celebration to mark *the event* that made the man famous rather than simply marking his birth or death. That event, of course, was the arrival of the three caravelles of Columbus's first flotilla—the *Niña*, the *Pinta*, and the *Santa Maria*—as the initial step in a great chain of progress leading to the birth of American democracy, and free public education as one of democracy's greatest fruits. Proposals to establish a similar celebration of Columbus's discovery today would inevitably be more controversial, given the broadening awareness of the record of brutal mistreatment by Columbus and his successors of the native peoples of the Americas, and an understanding that the arrival of the Europeans represented a genocidal catastrophe for indigenous civilizations.

At the time, however, Daniel Ford recognized Upham's idea as another inspired one, perhaps on a par with the Flag Over the Schoolhouse program. A Columbus commemoration in schools around the country would be an opportunity to nurture patriotic awareness among the young and, by piggybacking on the enormous publicity already being generated for the Chicago expo, to reap a promotional bonanza for the *Companion*. (More than twenty-seven million visitors would eventually pass through turnstiles at the Columbian Exposition grounds.)

Upham's brainchild was an early example of a promotional gambit that today might be called "event marketing." The goal of sponsoring organizations is to shine in the light of the prestige, the esteem, and the attention surrounding high-profile happen-

ings, whether sports spectacles like the Olympics and the Super-
bowl, or more modest events like fund-raising walks and charity
art shows. One example of event marketing written up in business school case studies is the campaign by the American Express
Company around the 1986 centennial of the Statue of Liberty. In
exchange for pledging money toward restoration of the statue,
the company earned the right to link its name to one of the most
cherished national monuments. The company rolled out this
privilege in marketing, advertising, public relations, lobbying, at
VIP receptions, and in almost any other way they could think of.

Even by today's standards, it is hard to imagine a more resounding success than what the *Youth's Companion*'s national
Columbus Day school commemoration turned out to be. Beyond
achieving high-profile promotion in schools around the country,
the program even turned a profit. In an archive at the University
of Rochester I found a simple accounting put together following the event. It reads:

$6,489.94	EXPENSES
$8,116.56	SALE OF FLAGS FOR THE EVENT
$1,626.62	PROFIT

Appended to the tally is an unsigned commentary exulting
that the *Companion* had "conducted what has proved to be the
most monumental piece of advertising ever attempted by a paper,
without one dollar of expense to itself; rather, with an actual
running profit from the incidentals created by the work." (The
sixteen-hundred-dollar net would be worth about forty thousand
dollars today.) When I came across the financial tally, I remarked
to Mary Huth, the librarian in charge of the archive, how surprising it was to find that the context of the Pledge's creation
was so commercial. "Yes," she said cheerfully, "but how very
American."

Back in early 1891, when the event was still just a gleam in

Upham's eye, the Columbus anniversary pageant's ultimate success was anything but certain. It was a stroke of good fortune that Charles C. Bonney, a key Columbian Exposition official, had also come up with the idea for some kind of school-based event. When he heard about Upham's idea, he readily approved Upham's proposal and anointed the *Companion* as the official sponsor.

With the Exposition's imprimatur in hand, Daniel Ford next landed the crucial support of Education Commissioner Harris. A Yale dropout, leading Hegelian scholar, and founder of *The Journal of Speculative Philosophy,* Harris was a former superintendent of schools in St. Louis, where he established the first public school kindergarten in 1873. He was also "a tireless crusader for universal public education," according to education historian Diane Ravitch, and "argued unceasingly that the purpose of education was to give the individual the accumulated wisdom of the human race, and that this was a public purpose fully deserving the support of the entire community." Harris personally backed the *Companion*'s plan and lined up the National Association of School Superintendents and the National Education Association to take part. The backing of these organizations added another official stamp to the plan and provided a national network for promoting the ceremony among teachers, students, and school administrators.

To help the busy premiums director organize the program and move it forward, Ford appointed the newly hired Francis Bellamy. A Baptist minister, Bellamy, then thirty-six, had recently left his job as pastor of Boston's Bethany Baptist Church, where Ford was a prominent member of the congregation. With Harris's blessing, Bellamy was named chairman of a steering committee set up to oversee the event, cementing the *Companion*'s control. "It was a staggering commitment for a young man untrained in wide affairs," Bellamy later wrote, "and I accepted it with trembling."

4. THE REVEREND FRANCIS BELLAMY

The trajectory of Francis Bellamy's life and role in American history may seem predestined. But in his time, it was an improbable journey from the far reaches and anonymity of western New York, where he was born and lived most of his first three decades, to Boston, where he would earn his lasting fame. It was an age of great quarrel and contradiction, of religious awakenings and heady materialism, as well as massive migrations and mergings of people and ideas. Bellamy may have seemed the unlikeliest of men to pull off an assignment to run a national marketing campaign, but in late-nineteenth-century America, he was also the perfect man for the job.

We know this: he came from sturdy stock. His mother, Lucy Eells, was born in a log cabin in 1819 near the Genesee River in Rochester, then just a tiny village of a few hundred people in what were still the wild and forested frontier lands of western New York. When her parents decided to seek a better future in an even more remote Michigan, they left young Lucy in the care of an aunt and uncle—and never returned for her.

This was the time—and place—when modern industry, in the form of the Erie Canal, which opened six years after Lucy's birth, met *The Last of the Mohicans,* published a year later and celebrating an era that was fast disappearing. The mighty hand-hewn waterway—363 miles of deep ditch dug out of rock and mud—would cut through American Indian lands, adding to the pressure on the tribes to move west or die. The canal was not just a symbol of the new nation's vigor, it added to that force, opening what was then the western frontier to easy transportation and the commerce that came with it. By 1830, Rochester had ninety-two hundred people and was, thanks to an abundance of waterfalls on the Genesee and a canal that cut transportation costs by over 90 percent, a humming hub of flour mills. By 1838 the city had doubled its population and was the largest flour-producing city in America—and arguably the nation's first "boomtown." It was the first of many such booms in America's push westward, that transformed towns and cities all along the canal route between Albany and Buffalo.

The canal was also a thoroughfare of ideas—"the Internet of its era," as commentator David Ronan put it many years later. Much of central and western New York became an epicenter of political and ideological ferment. And it put the region in the grip of the spiritual revival movement then in full flower. The Second Great Awakening, as it has been dubbed, was one of several periods of intense Christian evangelism in a country that was, and still is, whipsawing between high secularism and fervid religiosity. Historians have put the bookend dates on this Awakening at 1790 and 1840, a period of time when Francis Bellamy's parents were growing up in a region where the new evangelism enjoyed many adherents, including Joseph Smith, Jr., who claimed to have had his first "vision" of God on a hill near Manchester, New York, just thirty miles east of Rochester and on the Erie Canal. Smith said an angel named Moroni had given him a set of golden plates, which he translated and published in 1830, describing the hill as a place where, centuries earlier, 230,000 Nephite soldiers were killed in a final battle with the Lamanites.

And side by side with this intense spiritualism, equally intense political crusaders were gathering. In 1847, Frederick Douglass, the former slave, founded the abolitionist newspaper *The North Star* in Rochester, and the following year he attended the first women's rights convention in nearby Seneca Falls. This convention, and its resulting Declaration of Sentiments, marks what most historians now call the birth of the women's rights movement in the United States.

In 1855, when Francis Bellamy was born in Mount Morris, New York, twenty-five miles south of Rochester, the region was a bubbling cauldron of progressive social, religious, and political activism and upheaval. In this mix it is perhaps not surprising that Francis's mother, from pioneer stock, married a child of old New England. David Bellamy was the oldest of four sons born to a dry-goods merchant in Kingsbury, New York, not far from Lake George. David had passed up an offer by his father to go to college, accepting instead a thousand dollars to start his own business. He set up shop in a tiny village in the country town of Ellery, near Lake Chautauqua and Lake Erie, with his first wife, Eliza Benedict. But after only a few years of commerce, he was called to a religious life and was ordained a Baptist minister, like his great-grandfather Joseph and younger brother Rufus. Joseph Bellamy, a Yale graduate, was a preacher, author, and theologian of some note in the latter part of the eighteenth century. He was a student, and eventually friend, of the great evangelizer and religious thinker Jonathan Edwards, who is credited with igniting the (first) Great Awakening, an American religious resurgence—more determinedly practical than the Second—that began in the 1730s and ran up to the American Revolution, which was in part inspired by it. (Rufus's son Edward was to become famous as the author of *Looking Backward*.)

Self-educated though he was, David was a gifted preacher and was soon serving as pastor of two New York City churches. But after overseeing the establishment and construction of Hope Chapel, which later became Calvary Baptist Church on 57th Street in Manhattan, David suffered a health crisis—there is some evidence to suggest it was a nervous breakdown—and, at age forty-four, took refuge in his brother Frederick's home upstate.

He and his wife Eliza remained there for two years, until David grew strong enough to pastor a church in the nearby town of Arcadia, only to lose his wife to an illness.

Two years later, David married Lucy Ann Eells, fourteen years his junior, who had been a longtime friend of his first wife. He found another church, this one in Mount Morris, where Francis was born. Mount Morris sits near the northern end of the magnificent Letchworth gorge, which tourist brochures today call "the Little Grand Canyon." The twenty-two-mile-long chasm was carved over aeons by the Genesee, one of the country's few northward-flowing rivers, which drains into Lake Ontario, sixty-seven miles away. Francis's family departed Mount Morris when he was a young boy, but it is reasonable to suppose that, even for a five-year-old, a glimpse of the chasm—its rocky cliffs, its waterfalls, its thick forests—would have left imprinted in his mind's eye a landscape of grandeur and startling beauty. The young Francis may have been awed, too, by the raw power of the river, which regularly flooded the fields around Mount Morris and the town itself. (Today, a huge concrete dam, completed in 1952, helps control flooding.)

Unfortunately, within a few years of moving to Rome, just east of Seneca Falls, David died suddenly, of a stroke, at age fifty-eight. Francis was only nine years old. His uncle Rufus traveled from Northampton, Massachusetts, to help bury his brother, and the following Sunday mounted the pulpit of David's church to read the sermon the late pastor had prepared.

Despite his father's untimely death, young Frank excelled at the Rome Free Academy, the village's first public school, and was a member of the school's first graduating class—this at a time when there was great controversy over publicly funded schools, arguments that were still going on at the time of the *Youth's Companion* sponsorship of the national Columbus Day event in

1892. Francis no doubt owed much of his love of public school, a hallmark of that quadricentennial celebration, to his experience at the Rome Free Academy, and he later helped found the school's alumni association and served as its head.

It is tempting to speculate that for Francis Bellamy, fatherless from a young age, patriotism was in some way a surrogate, as the Greek root of the word suggests. Indeed, maybe anyone who gives themselves over to patriotic feeling is seeking a warm and protective parental embrace. In the case of Bellamy, the substitute-father theory might be plausible if patriotic activity had been an ongoing fixation for him, but in reality it wasn't. He could wax patriotic at the drop of a hat, especially when talking about the Pledge, but he was not exceptionally demonstrative on the subject.

To the extent that he had father surrogates, they were individual mentors, beginning with his father's successor as pastor of the Rome First Baptist Church. Francis was fifteen when the Reverend H. H. Peabody took over the pastorate in Rome. Peabody, an early adherent of Social Gospel belief, must have sowed a few seeds of dissent from mainstream religious notions within Francis's mind, a theological bent reinforced at Rochester Theological Seminary, founded as an alternate religious school in 1850, which Francis would later attend.

Still, Francis's mother must have been impressive. And Rome, the place Bellamy considered his hometown, no doubt played an important role in his formation. It is where he was schooled, where his mother continued to live until her death in 1898, where his ashes are enshrined. Redolent of history, the area was important for many generations. Called variously the Great Portage, or Oneida Carrying Place, or sometimes just Carry, it was where Indian travelers and traders had carried their canoes and their contents overland from the Mohawk River to Wood Creek, the sole connection from the Hudson River to Lake Ontario. Not far from Rome, at Fort Stanwix, the Third New York Regiment under the command of Colonel Peter Gansevoort held off a prolonged attack by British, German, Loyalist, Canadian, and American Indian troops under the command of British general Barry St. Leger in 1777. Following the Revolution, many of the soldiers that served at Fort Stanwix returned to the area, to live on the land nearby.

In the 1850s and 1860s, these rough-and-ready places were still very much part of a boy's life in a region that was part frontier, part economic and social mixing bowl. Francis was raised and educated in a region that felt the growing country's many surges keenly. And he came of age during the Civil War and Reconstruction, a time of tremendous national strife, only to see the country lose its way decades later when, as he put it, "the shameless, indecent, almighty dollar came in and turned the heads of our people from the contemplation of our better traditions."

All these currents fed a young mind that was also surrounded by books and religion. He was lucky to be educated at a new school and he had most surely heard his father pacing the family living room practicing his Sunday orations. He learned and became a practiced speaker. "A very natural orator is Frank J. Bellamy," said the Rome *Sentinel* newspaper following his high-school commencement address in July 1872. "The speaker possesses a very full and round voice, speaks fluently and distinctly, and appears upon the stage with most of the graces of a practiced orator." For his essay on Horace Greeley, one of two compositions awarded prizes, young Frank received a poetry collection that included works of Spencer, Dante, Chaucer, Milton, and Tasso.

At the University of Rochester, he also won essay prizes, both as a sophomore and as a senior. As a commencement orator in June 1876, the centennial year of the Declaration of Independence, Francis extolled the moral power of American poetry as a galvanizing force in opposition to slavery:

[It is] in the new world, in our own day, that the Poetry of Man has found its noblest mission. Here, in the birthplace of liberty, was heard the clank of the fetter, the despairing moan of a race of slaves. In America, the lash had drunk of human blood and the wail of the oppressed awaked response in America's finest poets—Longfellow, Lowell and Whittier. To arouse a nation from apathy, to stimulate to action, to reconquer Freedom was the Poet's mission.

While some of the twenty-one-year-old scholar's rhetoric may seem overwrought to twenty-first-century readers, a newspaper reporter covering the commencement judged the speech to be "one of the very finest" of the occasion. "The oration was carefully and elegantly written and delivered with great earnestness and power," the reporter wrote in a review of the commencement proceedings.

As a Baptist minister—first in the prosperous Mohawk valley town of Little Falls and later in Boston—Bellamy gained plenty of practice putting words together and became especially adept at phrasing ideas to be delivered orally—whether in formal sermons and invocations or extemporaneous remarks at the baptismal bath, at grace over meals, at the wedding bower, at the sick bed, the graveside, and in the multitude of other circumstances a man of the cloth is called on to say the right thing.

There is some irony in Francis Bellamy's flag salute having become an exercise in conformity. Bellamy himself was, from an early age, an independent-minded person, at times even a maverick. He was strong-willed with a robust intellect and the enterprise and initiative to chart his own course. While in Little Falls, according to John W. Bauer, a retired economics professor who has written a wonderful short history of the Pledge, he supported a presidential candidate of the National Prohibition Party against Republican James Blaine and Democrat Grover

Cleveland. But while there, as Margaret Butterfield of the University of Rochester archives says, Bellamy "devot[ed] much of his time to work with laboring people." Among everyday folk of the late nineteenth century, Bellamy would be as good a model as any of the "rugged individualist" whom historian Frederick Jackson Turner famously described in 1893 as the epitome of the American frontier experience. His "niece" Marian, the only daughter of his cousin Edward, described her "Uncle Frank" as a man with "rugged features to match his body. He was altogether charming and urbane, which qualities did not seem to fit his physical makeup."

This may have been what attracted Harriet Benton, a Methodist, to him. The young couple married in 1881, in Newark, New York, a town not far from where Francis's mother was born. Francis and Hattie would have two sons, John and David, and be together for thirty-seven years, until Hattie died in 1918. But just four years after they married the young couple moved to Boston, where Francis took up the pastoral reins of the Dearborn Street Church. As Ms. Butterfield points out, "again he distinguished himself as a leader in the movement to utilize the church as a means of social and educational as well as religious service." John Baer says that Francis "felt it was his duty to bring moral and spiritual uplift to hard-pressed factory workers and their families. He liked the idea of a church service for the poor which emphasized charity, philanthropy, education, and spiritual uplift. Labor disturbances were prominent in the news, and Francis wanted to help solve their economic, social, political and religious problems."

But though Bellamy was successful in building his flock at Dearborn Street, Irish immigration brought more Catholics to the neighborhood, and the young preacher was forced to move his congregation to a different part of the city and Bethany Baptist. His new congregants were not as sympathetic with Bellamy's increasingly socialist views. He was an outspoken advocate of the rights of working people and the equal distribution of economic resources, which he believed was inherent in the teachings of Jesus. Bellamy became a charter member of the First Nationalist Club in Boston, formed to discuss and implement the ideas in his cousin's bestselling *Looking Backward,* and was the vice president of education of the Society of Christian Socialists in Boston.

All of this was too much for Bethany's business establishment, which reduced funding for the church in the spring of 1891. For his part, Bellamy arrived at the conclusion that the ministry required "a spirit, a versatility, a tirelessness of pastoral care which he had no longer to give," and abruptly resigned. Years later, the congregation would remember him "as a man who brought to the service of communities a creative mind, a kindly heart and a just fame."

Though it is unclear what the majority of the congregation thought of Bellamy, it could not have been an easy decision for him. In his four years at Bethany Church, he had baptized the young, comforted the sick, buried the dead, consoled the bereaved, and soothed many a troubled soul. He had found a new home for the congregation when the old neighborhood tilted too Catholic, and he had gotten a new church built. With that kind of investment, it could not have been a trouble-free resignation. At the same time, though, leaving the pastorate seems to have been a relief and a release for Bellamy. He had been restive in the ministry for some time—weary of shepherding a flock and keen to test himself in a broader sphere. Now, though, he was unemployed with a wife and two sons to support and a new house half-built.

He was not long out of a job. Daniel Ford, a member of the Dearborn Street Church who had followed Bellamy to Bethany because he was sympathetic to the minister's philosophical beliefs and his oratory, offered him a job at the *Youth's Companion.* He saw talent, pluck, and practical energy in the raw-boned preacher from western New York. He had witnessed Bellamy get the new church built, he had heard his homilies and read his essays. And Ford had seen Bellamy hold his ground with the hidebound church hierarchy, even though it cost him his livelihood. He wanted to help Bellamy, and Ford, the hardheaded businessman, saw something in Bellamy he believed could help him.

As Bellamy moved on to the world of journalism, he took with him his passion for social justice and love of America; the ability to work within the confines of a structured institution (like the church) and get things done; and a great intellectual energy. He was committed to restoring American "principles" and "ideals" and would apply these considerable skills to that task.

5. A NATIONAL CELEBRATION

Diligent by nature, it was Bellamy's habit to tackle any task set before him with energy, determination, and high expectations. And whatever emotions roiled within him during this major career change, outwardly he conveyed confidence and determination as he undertook the task of organizing a nationwide salute to the discovery of America.

He already had a sense of the obstacles ahead of him. Coordinating the details and getting cooperation from all the necessary parties toward a single national event involving thousands of schools and millions of people would be no small feat.

It was the spring of 1892, with the October anniversary of the Columbian landfall fast approaching. Bellamy knew there was no time to stand on ceremony. He wrote two lengthy memos to his boss explaining what he had been doing and proposing a bold plan to keep "the Press" interested. So far, he told Ford, the Clipping Bureau had already found two hundred editorials about the October event. But "the fire is slackening." The second memo, especially, is a peek into the mind of a marketing man—no detail is unimportant. "It seems to me we shall want both a Morning and an Afternoon Celebration—each for different purposes," he tells Ford. "You see, we ask the schools to celebrate the Day, and we also ask the people to make the schools the center of Celebration. This double purpose cannot be accomplished at a single session, except in rural schools where the school-house is the great rallying place of the people. In towns and cities two occasions will be needful." Bellamy suggested that the schools have "their own exercises—for which we will furnish the program" and that "the citizens' celebration take place in the largest hall in the town, preceded by a procession in which the older pupils will be escorted by the veterans and by other organizations, this Afternoon Celebration to be distinctly keyed on the Public School note. Consequently, we shall need at least three varieties of Program. . . ."

But the real beauty of this six-page typewritten letter to Ford, dated April 18, 1892, is Bellamy's second section, "Pushing the Movement." It is here that he justifies Ford's confidence in giving him such a large responsibility. "The work thus far done has only launched the movement," Bellamy writes. "It requires a great deal more to make it an assured success." His analysis is straightforward and to the point. "General local apathy must get such repeated shakings that every locality will at last wake up and produce at least one man who will say, 'This thing must be done here.'" Bellamy then proceeds to outline a four-point plan for "repeated shakings," ending with what he warned was the "main dependence" for success: the press. "Success hangs on the amount and continuance of newspaper talk."

Newspaper talk? A thoroughly modern publicist at work.

Bellamy indeed knew the media. "It is only the concrete that appeals to the Daily Press," he tells Ford, "and it is hard to keep them supplied with concrete material. They will not publish our general effusions." Bellamy's frank and honest assessment must have appealed to Ford, the man who once followed the minister to his new church. "It is easy to foresee that shortly the great din of the Presidential Campaign will drown out our noise unless we make preparations for keeping our rumble going," he continued, correctly assessing what would be a historic confrontation between Grover Cleveland, itching for retribution, and then-President Benjamin Harrison, who had, in 1888, prevented Cleveland from having a second term. "I believe we can do this," said Bellamy. "But we must do it by giving concrete news to the Press."

How did he propose to give such news to the Press?

"I have a special plan to submit to you for the making of this kind of news," he said:

> The Dailies will publish, and comment on, what leading statesmen say. What Mr. Blaine, Mr. Cleveland, Mr. Reed, Mr. McKinley etc. think about this plan would be telegraphed everywhere, printed, and commented on editorially. Such men, who would not allow themselves to be "interviewed," would talk with me as the Chairman of this great movement and would allow me to give "currency to their opinions."
>
> So I want to ask you if this would not be the best step now;—
>
> Let me go on to Washington taking letters from Gov. Russell to our Massachusetts Senators and Representatives asking their cordial endorsement and introduction since this is a *Boston idea*.

Bellamy was clearly no country rube, with no small ambition to "see the leading men in Washington, including the President." And he left no stone unturned: the ten-day trip would be cost effective. "It would cost about $75.00," he told Ford. "But that amount might otherwise quickly be spent in printing and postage which would not achieve anywhere near the same result."

Ford was convinced. And his considerable connections would undoubtedly serve Bellamy's cause, greasing the wheels and opening doors, including that of the influential Republican congressman from Massachusetts, Henry Cabot Lodge. An appointment at the White House soon came through.

Bellamy charged down to Washington, but not without

shrewdly stopping first in New York to secure the support of the once (and future) president Grover Cleveland. In the election of 1888, Cleveland, the incumbent, had beaten the challenger Harrison in the popular vote—only to lose in the electoral college when the Tammany Hall machine helped tip New York State's decisive thirty-four votes into the Republican column. Now Cleveland was preparing to try to take back the presidency for the Democrats in the 1892 balloting.

At the White House, Congressman Lodge introduced Bellamy to President Harrison, letting it be known that Cleveland had already promised support. Harrison quickly agreed to back the Columbus school commemoration and promised to write a letter of endorsement. But Bellamy also conducted one of his many interviews—this was "the concrete material" the press would love—with the president. Harrison told him that he was "interested in all that pertains to the Public School and I like to see the Flag over the School." Already in campaign mode, he reminded Bellamy that "I did as much as anyone to promote the School Flag idea." But Harrison's limitations were apparent. "The best thing to do with [these flags] is for these business men to give them to the Public Schools to be a perpetual lesson in patriotism," he told Bellamy. Harrison was probably less a marketing man than Bellamy. "They used to think that all the school had to do was to teach the '3 Rs' as we called it out West," the president continued. "But they see it differently now, and it is time. The school is the place for education in intelligent patriotism and citizenship."

Harrison was proud of his support for public education and it was clear that Bellamy and Upham had done the right thing by making the schools the central sponsor of their Columbus event. "Yes, I talked this from Maine to California," said Harrison. "I told the people twenty times along the route, that the American free education system was the choicest institution we had."

Then he stopped. "I've said enough on this subject, Mr. Bellamy," he abruptly concluded, advising the magazine man to "present the matter to me in writing or printing so that I can see it before me easily, and I will call in my stenographer and dictate a few sentences which will cover the ground you want."

As the president tendered a farewell handshake, Bellamy stuck a verbal foot in the door. "I thank you, Mr. President," said the cheeky former preacher, "but I was going to ask you if you wouldn't issue a proclamation making the day a national holiday and recommending the people to observe it in the public schools." The president stiffened and Lodge glared at Bellamy. "Why sir," said Harrison, "that is impossible without congressional authority."

Lodge hustled Bellamy out. "That was going too far after the president showed you such consideration," Lodge scolded. "You almost tipped over the apple cart." Bellamy was contrite, but only momentarily. "I'm sorry if I made a bull," he said. "Now we'll have to get Congress to give him the authority."

"That is absolutely impractical," Lodge sputtered. He reminded Bellamy, with what patience he could muster, that the Democrats, who controlled the House, would never allow Harrison to hand voters an extra day off from work during an election year. "But I didn't know any better than to try," Bellamy later reminisced.

And so Bellamy began to haunt the halls of Congress, interviewing, or trying to, dozens of Capitol Hill solons. Some legislators sidestepped the issue completely. Senator David B. Hill (D.-N.Y.), harboring presidential fantasies, declined comment. Senator John Sherman (R.-Ohio), chair of the Foreign Relations Committee, said he was too busy worrying about external affairs to have an opinion. With others, though, Bellamy found success. Rather than arm-twist the lawmakers, he asked for "interviews," ostensibly to gather their assessments of the proposed Columbus Day commemoration. How would it be received in the West? he asked a senator from South Dakota. What was the view from Texas? he asked another. What would a Southern senator think about including Civil War veterans, "both the Blue and the Gray"? One by one, influential lawmakers embraced the idea of a national Columbus celebration in public schools as if it were their own. Congressman William Holman (D.-Ind.) called the plan "an admirable one," and was much impressed that the event "is calculated to sweep the whole country. Nothing can withstand the force of it."

"Where do you think, Judge Holman, that the Celebration will be most successful?" Bellamy asked.

"It will prevail most among the country schools," replied Holman, "in the real country schools at the crossroads and in the back country. . . . The country people are almost as quick to read the news of the day as the people in the cities who have the daily papers, but there is this difference; what they read in their weekly papers certainly makes a deeper impression upon them."

It is clear from reading Bellamy's transcripts of these interviews that he had a list of questions—at least, subjects—that he wanted to cover. But the language of his subjects is far from pat, with clear and oftentimes remarkably trenchant comments from the country's "leading men" at an important period of American history.

One common theme, which seems almost quaint today, is the significance of Columbus and his "discovery." "The voyage of Columbus was made in the name of enlightenment and progress, in spite of ignorance and conservatism," said Congressman Durborow (D.-Ill.). "It is also peculiarly appropriate because our free educational system is the direct product of what Columbus stood for," added Lodge. "Whatever may be said of Columbus, he certainly stood as a protest against ignorance. He achieved his discovery in spite of all that ignorance could do to defeat him. His protest against ignorance and the general spirit of enlightenment, which has always been the spirit of this country, are one and the same. Of course the Public School ought to lead in the Celebration. What is the program to be?"

And many of the legislators drew a quick line between the enlightenment that Columbus represented and the role of public schools in the celebration. "There is a direct line of connection between the determination of Columbus to break through the limitations of the Middle Ages and the educational system which represents the modern spirit of enlightenment," said Durborow. Even Congressman Joseph Bailey (D.-Tex.), who announced that he was "uncompromisingly opposed to the appropriation of a single dollar more for that Exposition" and was "hostile to this sort of thing from first to last," was very much in favor of the Public School Celebration. "It not only asks for no money from the Government, but most of all, and best of all, it centers itself in the hearts of the people. . . . It depends entirely upon the people of each locality, and in that respect it represents the American idea. . . . It will be an object lesson in the responsibilities of citizenship."

There was no doubt, at least among the several dozen or so congressmen that Bellamy interviewed, that education was an important subject. "When the children begin to take an interest in historical matters the rest of the world has to follow," said Congressman Sherman Hoar (D.-Mass.). "Children can make anything in the world interesting, and significant as well." "Our perpetuity as a Nation depends upon the education of all the citizens," exclaimed Mr. Bailey of Texas. "That is the one line where individual liberty must give way to the general good. No man has a right to demand that his children shall grow up ignorant. No man who has property has the right to deny the advantages of education to the children of the man who has no property." Congressman Roger Mills (D.-Tex.), seemed to make a similar exception to the preeminence of individual, or states', rights when it came to education. "The Public School cannot be exalted too much," he told Bellamy. "You must remember it is a state institution and not a national one." That notwithstanding, Mills continued, "A mass of ignorant citizens is always a menace to justice and liberty. Therefore we must take the public money, and compel these children to be educated."

"Our public school system is what makes this Nation superior to all other Nations—not the Army or Navy system," said Hoar. "Military display . . . does not belong here." In fact, a number of the congressmen expressed their desire to keep the military, except for the Grand Army, a group of Civil War veterans from the North, out of this. "I have no patience with all this Naval Display and Military Display for Columbus Day," intoned Congressman William Campbell Preston Breckinridge (D.-Ky.), a former colonel in the Confederate Army. "What place has it in that day? We have had war enough. The genius of the country isn't arms and military display. . . . [W]e are made for different things. Our progress lies in the direction of enlightenment, and that is what the Public School stands for. The Children ought to be made to feel on that day that enlightenment and not the showiness of uniforms, and the perfection of machines for killing men, is the real destiny of this land of ours. They can't learn that too early either."

An interesting exception to the general roll of interviewees was Theodore Roosevelt, then serving as president of the U.S. Civil Service Commission. Bellamy clearly recognized the political clout that the young Harrison appointee from New York had. And Roosevelt didn't disappoint:

> Yes, I believe in the Celebration of Columbus Day, by the Public Schools of America, from the word "go." The public School is the keystone of the arch of our civilization. It stands for the American principle of equality. It is a great thing to give to the average man

the principles of progress and enlightenment. Other nations have given these privileges to a few; we have given them to all. And so the Public School, perhaps more truly than any other institution in America, represents the essential moral spirit.

This 400th anniversary ought to be made more of than any other Centennial in history. The Discovery of America was the first step in the revolution of the whole world. It has already brought two Americas and Australia into the civilized world. It set in motion the chain of energies which has opened up Asia and Africa to civilization. The Old World civilization clustered around the Mediterranean Sea; in the Middle Ages civilization centered in Europe; but now civilization is world-wide. No other one thing has been so important in the history of our race, as we know it, as the Discovery of America. It has made possible this world-wide civilization.

The part the Flag is to play, in this Celebration of the 12th of October, appeals to me tremendously. We are all the descendants from emigrants, but we want to hasten the day, by every possible means, when we shall be fused together in an entire and new race, or rather the new races of a new world. Consequently, by all means in our power we ought to inculcate, among the children of this country, the most fervent loyalty to the Flag.

The Common School and the Flag stand together as archtypical of American civilization. The Common School is the leading form in which the principles of equality and fraternity take shape; while the Flag represents not only these principles of equality, fraternity and liberty, but also the great pulsing nation with all its hopes, and all its past, and all its moral power. So it is eminently fitting that the Common School and the Flag should stand out together on Columbus Day.

I am particularly pleased with this Celebration by the Public Schools when I look at it from the national standpoint. It will mean that we are all one people. The South, as well as the North, will join heartily in it. It will signalize as no local observance could do, and as no general observance base on any other institution could do, the fact that we are a solid nation.

Within a few weeks, Bellamy's Capitol Hill lobbying paid off. Congress approved a joint resolution empowering the president to proclaim a national holiday "with suitable exercises in schools." Despite that victory, though, the White House proved maddeningly slow to issue a proclamation. President Harrison's reputation for fretting and dawdling over even minor administrative details seemed to be accurate. Bellamy needed the official proclamation to begin convincing state governors to follow suit with decrees of their own.

The real hold up, however, came from Capitol Hill and not from the White House. An argument had surfaced within Congress centering around whether the proclamation should set the date for Columbus Day as October 12 or October 21.

Though there was a scholarly question over the historically correct date for the actual Columbus landing, some observers believed that politics had something to do with the reconsideration as well, as the number of VIP speakers for events on October 12 was limited. And for a brief moment the tempest in the teacup grew into a maelstrom that almost sucked the school celebration down.

The scholarly argument revolved around the change in worldwide calendar use from the Julian calendar to the Gregorian calendar beginning in 1582, some ninety years after the Columbus landing. While the original written entry in Columbus's log set the landing date in 1492 as October 12, the adoption of the Gregorian calendar prompted many people to revisit historical dates. The change, based on sixteenth-century recalculations, improved on the Julian calendar because it accommodated for the actual length of the solar year, which is not a perfect 365 days. The Gregorian calendar introduced the leap year every four years, adding a day into the year, to keep the counting of days almost nearly accurate. In 1582 the Catholic church literally made up for lost time by readjusting the calendar in that year and declaring that the day that followed October 5, 1582, would be October 15, thereby catching up on ten days that the Julian calendar had not properly accounted for.

This historic shift in dates was what consumed the thoughts of some members of Congress in 1892. After all, Columbus set foot in the Americas on October 12 of the Old Style calendar, not the new. This strictness of historical dates gathered adherents within Congress to move to change the date for the observation of Columbus Day, or "Discovery Day."

The controversy about Gregorian versus Julian calendars had not been resolved throughout the world in 1892. Many countries by that date had not adopted the Gregorian calendar. In fact, it would not be until 1929 that worldwide adoption of a single calendar—the Gregorian—was achieved. Until that time, world travelers would go from one country to another and literally not know what day it was. Part of the problem with the adoption of the Gregorian calendar is that its original source was a decree by a Catholic pope. Non-Catholic countries had no interest in this new calendar. For example, non-Catholic England and its colonies, including, of course, the American colonies, did not adopt the Gregorian calendar until 1752. By that time there was an *eleven*-day difference between the Old Style

Julian calendar and the Gregorian system. The official change within England and its possessions took place in September of 1752; the day that followed September 2, 1752, was September 14, 1752. All old dates were readjusted to fit the new system. So, for example, George Washington's birthday, which was February 11, 1732, suddenly jumped to February 22 during the year 1753, as it is noted on the calendar today.

For Bellamy, the arguments over the precise historic date to mark the Columbus landing proved infuriating. He had a deadline to meet and needed an official date, whatever it might be, to focus the *Companion*'s school events around. Congress, and more significantly congressional staff members, dithered back and forth over the issue as precious weeks melted away.

Bellamy himself wanted to stay with the October 12 date in part because the *Companion* had already announced that October 12 was the date for the celebration, but also because large-scale events had already been announced and planned on that date for New York City and for the groundbreaking ceremonies for the Columbian Exposition in Chicago.

But punctilious members of Congress continued to press the importance of strict historic correctness by refusing to allow the United States of America to officially declare any date but October 21 as the date of the Columbus landing—noting that in 1492 the difference between a Julian calendar date and a reconsidered date under the Gregorian calendar would have been nine days.

Back and forth the calendar argument went, until it looked like the entire enterprise might end in a stalemate. With the "21" camp refusing to bend, Bellamy finally gave in, bowing to the need for a timely congressional resolution.

As June turned toward July, Bellamy again descended on the executive mansion, where he learned that paperwork for the proclamation had gone to the State Department where it had stalled for weeks.

"I immediately called upon Secretary of State [John] Foster

and asked him if the proclamation might not be hurried," Bellamy later wrote. Secretary Foster, in his cabinet post less than a month, was about to show the presumptuous magazine factotum the door when an assistant came in to report that the order for the proclamation had just been received. Seizing the moment, Bellamy pressed the issue with a velveteen coyness that might have made Machiavelli blush. "I thought that possibly I was in a position to contribute one or two valuable points of view as to [the proclamation's] phrasing," he recounted years later. "I gave as my only excuse that in view of the coming election a tactful wording of that proclamation was very important, and that . . . the whole matter up till now had resulted from personal conferences with Congressional leaders and the President himself. . . ."

Whether exasperated or convinced, Foster decided to put the ball back in Bellamy's court. "I'll send you right up to the Third Assistant Secretary, Mr. Creidler, and he will give you the form and you can write out the first draft yourself," said the secretary of state. Bellamy set down a draft. Perfectly aligning the first national Columbus Day celebration to the *Youth's Companion* vision, the declaration peaked with this pneumatic passage: "*Let the National Flag float over every schoolhouse in the country, and the exercises be such as shall impress upon our youth the patriotic duties of citizenship.*" The next day, newspapers carried the president's official decree with Bellamy's text intact.

And so, the first official national observance of Columbus Day fell on October 21. As we know today, subsequent decisions about the date to observe fell back to the traditional date of October 12. In the early part of the twentieth century a number of states started declaring official Columbus Day commemorative days—all on October 12. Then, in 1934, after strong lobbying by the Knights of Columbus, President Franklin Roosevelt declared Columbus Day a federal holiday—again, on October 12. All the scholarly precision that vexed Bellamy in 1892 became

even more irrelevant in 1971 when the holiday was fixed to the
second Monday in October—making a specific historic connection to a specific date less important than the convenience of
a set three-day holiday weekend. (Coincidentally, the second
Monday in October is celebrated in Canada as Thanksgiving.)

While the first *national* date for Columbus Day was set for
October 21, the complex and elaborate festivities in New York
City remained firmly committed for October 12. The organizers of the groundbreaking ceremonies at the Columbian Exposition in Chicago, on the other hand, embraced the new October
21 date. They had been concerned that dignitaries who were
scheduled to attend the events on October 12 in New York City
would not come to Chicago. Now, however, with a nine-day
separation between the two events, the same dignitaries could
attend both, which they did.

With the first national Columbus Day commemoration now
officially proclaimed, Bellamy had three months to attract
enough local participation around the country to make the
school event truly national in scope. The main vehicle for getting the word out was the *Youth's Companion* itself. Ads ran for
weeks promoting both the school celebration and the ongoing
school flag campaign to its hundreds of thousands of readers:

> Has *your* school yet obtained its Flag for this great
> Celebration? [One ad asked readers in large bold
> type.] Ask your Teacher to send for our Flag Certifi-
> cates. By the sale of these Flag Certificates for 10
> cents each to the friends of the pupils, your school
> can raise money for its Flag in one day.

Copy for another ad said:

> $3.50 will buy a bunting flag of best quality, 6 feet
> long, just right for a "little country school," and for

$5.35 a flag 9 feet long. . . . The boys can cut the flag-staff.

In the weeks that followed, Bellamy led a juggernaut campaign of promotion and public relations. He inveigled governors to issue proclamations in their own states and urged the head of the Grand Army of the Republic, the fraternal organization of Civil War veterans, to get former troops from both sides involved. He sent brochures and personal letters to school superintendents. He sent streams of correspondence to newspaper editors offering ready-made editorials and news features already typeset and cast in boilerplate. (The promotional instincts, creativity, and resourcefulness he displayed would eventually come in handy during his later career in advertising.)

Meanwhile, Bellamy and James Upham were assembling a "programme" for the ceremony, to be published in the *Companion* and sent out in bulk to schools. The order of ceremony reflected an era when audiovisual technology had yet to make an appearance. There were no amps and loudspeakers, no theatrical lighting, no satellite hookups, no Quicktime videos, no Power Point slides, no digital effects. In the arena of public gatherings, it was still very much an acoustic era and the impact of a presentation relied on the unaided projection of the human voice, on movement, and on gesture.

The day would feature American flags in front of public school buildings in every community. The flood of patriotic expression would crystallize when children across the country stood and saluted the flag. The special recitation would be followed by several other works that were commissioned for this extraordinary day.

Poetry, celebratory song, readings, and formal addresses were common components of most any ceremonial gathering in American towns and cities. Declamation and group recitations were standard fare, especially in any assembly having to do with patriotism and civic life. "Oratory is the parent of liberty," said a handbook on public speaking popular at the time. The Columbus Day program to be published in the *Companion* for schools around the country to follow would feature a reading of President Harrison's proclamation, a group singing of "America" ("My Country 'tis of Thee"), and a prayer or scripture reading. The *Companion* had also commissioned a song by Theron Brown ("*Hail him who thro' darkness first followed the Flame / that led where the Mayflower of Liberty came*") and an ode by Edna Dean Proctor ("*Blazon Columbia's emblem, / The bounteous, golden Corn! / Eons ago, of the great sun's glow / And the joy of the earth, 'twas born*"). No one seemed to think that any of these original pieces might achieve popularity beyond the 1892 event.

An oration, "The Meaning of Four Centuries," had been assigned to W.C.P. Breckinridge, known as "the silver tongue of Kentucky." But two drafts from the renowned speaker had proved unsatisfactory to Daniel Ford. He threw the task to the busy Bellamy who, drawing on a facility honed through years of penning weekly homilies, dashed off a speech, which Ford okayed. ("*Four hundred years ago this morning, the Pinta's gun broke the silence, and announced the discovery of this hemisphere. . . .*")

Of all the elements in the program, the one accorded the dramatic focus of the ceremony was the raising of the Stars and Stripes, accompanied by a formal Salute to the Flag, to be recited by the students. As the deadline approached to send the program to press, this one key component remained unwritten. The salute was "the nub of the program," Bellamy later quipped, "and the nub was the rub."

A flag salute did exist at the time and was in common use. It had been composed by Colonel George T. Balch, a Civil War veteran and New York City school teacher, who devised it in conjunction with the first Flag Day celebration in 1885. The Balch

Salute ran: *"I give my heart and my hand to my country—one country, one language, one flag."* At his death in 1895, Balch was "famous for his work in awakening a feeling of patriotism in school children," according to *The New York Times*. "His plan was to have flag poles raised on all school houses in the land."

The Balch Salute had gained some popularity in the public schools. Bellamy, however, dismissed it as "too juvenile." He and Upham wanted to replace Balch's constricting text with a salute "of more dignity" that, in Bellamy's words, "carried more historical meaning." Amid the frenetic preparations for the October event, Bellamy and Upham had thrown the job of writing the salute back and forth for weeks. Upham tried his hand, jotting drafts at the breakfast table day after day, but the right words didn't come. Bellamy would later say that his idea for the new salute was a "straight-out vow of allegiance." The word "allegiance" was a playback to the Civil War, which still seared popular memory.

Eventually there arrived a day in August, the precise date nowhere recorded, when the printer's press deadline loomed the following morning. Upham and Bellamy stayed late at the *Companion* that evening. They talked through ideas for the salute over supper at the nearby Thorndike Hotel, then strolled back to the office at 201 Columbus Avenue through the heat of a summer evening. Ultimately, Upham pressed the task of actually composing the salute on his energetic colleague. "You write it," Bellamy remembered him insisting. "You have a knack at words."

Bellamy asked Upham to stay around to review what he came up with. He went to his desk, loosened his stiff collar, then took up a lead pencil and a piece of scrap paper. The evening was still sweltering, even though a breeze wafted in off Boston Harbor.

After what he later recalled was "two sweating hours," Bellamy emerged from his office, called Upham, and read aloud to him the twenty-two-word draft he had settled on: *I pledge allegiance to my Flag and the Republic for which it stands, one nation, indivisible, with liberty and justice for all.*

As Bellamy later recalled, "After the first phrase, 'I pledge allegiance to my Flag,' the rest was arduous mental labor."

He described his thinking process in detail some thirty years later:

"Allegiance to the Flag"—Why? Because it stands for something concrete behind it. What is that concrete background?

"The Republic." That word *Republic,* however, is perhaps too concrete, with little natural appeal to a child. What then is this Republic?

It is the whole Nation. We are still near the earlier days when the wholeness of the Nation had been disputed. So the words *one* and *indivisible* came to mind—words made familiar by Webster and Lincoln and made vital by the Civil War. That was the genesis of the phrase "and the Republic for which it stands, one Nation indivisible."

And what is the purpose and aim of this indivisible Nation? The first thought was of the phrase which Jefferson had brought back from the French Revolution, "liberty, equality, fraternity." But that was discarded as too remote and too impossible of realization.

What then? *Liberty* and *justice* came as the answer, with a final *for all.*

In the hands of a less skilled and experienced writer than Francis Bellamy, the flag salute that we now know as the Pledge of Allegiance might have quickly disappeared into oblivion. That it came into common use is attributable at least in part to its being (in its original form) a clean, easy-flowing, and pleasantly cadenced piece of writing. The kind of compact prose that trips off the tongue as the Pledge does is deceptively difficult to craft. Once accomplished, it seems simple, which is a hallmark of effective composition.

Both the quality of the writing and the care that went into it were characteristic of Bellamy. As eager as he must have been to complete this final program element for the Columbus Day school commemoration and get out of the office on an uncomfortably hot night, we can be sure that there was nothing haphazard about Bellamy's approach to composing the flag salute on that August evening. He was a conscientious wordsmith and no doubt weighed every word, scribbled and crumpled one draft after another until he was well satisfied with the content and the phrasing.

Conveying thoughts clearly, cleanly, and efficiently was a facility Bellamy would hone under the keen tutelage of Daniel Ford, publisher of *Youth's Companion*. "Mr. Ford," Bellamy remarked many years later, "was one of the finest masters of English I ever met. . . . His own blue pencil was my merciless censor." But that night, having been with the *Companion* for barely a year, it was probably not Ford's tutelage that had much effect, but the voices of preachers past.

The complete "Official Programme," including the original wording of the Pledge, was published in the September 8, 1892, issue of the *Companion*.

In later years, Bellamy and the *Companion* claimed that thousands of local communities and millions of schoolchildren participated in the publication's observance of its "Official Programme." Certainly school participation picked up momentum following reports of the hugely successful Columbus Day events in New York City on October 12. Throngs of people lined the streets to watch the parade in New York and more throngs gathered to listen to speeches and bands celebrating with popular music.

But it is unknown exactly how precisely all the various schools followed the *Companion*'s script on the official national date of October 21. While many newspapers made note of the school observation ceremonies, the only community that can be certain to have followed the "programme" to the letter was Malden, Massachusetts—the hometown of James B. Upham. Bellamy was on hand in Malden to witness this accurate unfolding of the *Companion*'s "Official Programme." And he himself gave a speech to the gathered crowd.

After hearing the Pledge recited aloud on that day by schoolchildren, Bellamy felt that the rhythm wasn't exactly right. He thought hard about it, parsing the sentence over and over until finally deciding what was wrong: there should be an additional "to" in front of "the Republic." The change was made immediately and from that day, until the next time the Pledge was altered in 1923, the Pledge stood at twenty-three words.

In today's version of the Pledge, which has nine additional words, the elegant architecture of the original text is still visible, and the fundamental themes still shine through. Bellamy packed a lot of meaning into that single sentence. But how, during those hours of fervid scribbling and scratching out, did the ideas in the Pledge find their way to the page? To begin to answer that question, it will be helpful to know what shaped the man behind the ideas.

6. I PLEDGE ALLEGIANCE:
THE FABRIC OF LIFE

Francis Bellamy may have possessed the exceptional writing talent needed to compose the Pledge, but the idea (and necessity) for a patriotic salute to the flag was not unique. The "flag-raising movement," as it was known, was well under way when Bellamy joined *Youth's Companion* in 1891.

By then the *Companion* was a national family paper read by parents and teachers as well as children, the *Life* magazine of its day. It produced 52 issues a year, published 7 book-length serials, 50 lead stories, 150 "special contributions," 260 good short stories, 1,000 brief notes, and 2,000 anecdotes, poems, and humorous sketches. Each new subscription included 10 issues and a calendar "in 12 colors and gold." At the time Bellamy penned the pledge, the *Companion* had a circulation of 500,000.

The ideas, the style, and the feeling of the words Bellamy set down in the Pledge were a product of his time, to be sure, but also, more particularly, his life experience, his intellectual and philosophical journey, his ideals and prejudices all are the sources of the Pledge. Like many of his peers, Bellamy feared the new generation was losing touch with the extraordinary sacrifice of the Civil War generation.

But why a push to salute or pledge allegiance to the flag at this particular time—in the late nineteenth century?

Anxiety over increasing immigration loomed large at that time and men like Bellamy, George Balch, and James Upham were concerned about the country's future and identity. The wave of immigration that occurred during the late 1890s brought people "who looked different"—from southern and eastern Europe—as well as large numbers of Catholics and Jews.

Bellamy was also concerned about the "enemy within," immigrants or native-born Americans who were "not patriotic enough."

It is unclear whether Bellamy thought he was writing for the ages when he penned the Pledge. But after the practice of reciting it spread during the early years of the twentieth century, he became more outspoken about it, including defending his authorship of it. In the wake of World War I and the Russian Revolution, he discussed using the Pledge to help combat internal subversion. He viewed the Pledge as "an inoculation" against the "virus" of radical thought and subversion. And he could not escape the "melting pot" issues of his time,★ as is clear from these ruminations written several years after he wrote the Pledge:

> The hard, inescapable fact is that men [are] not born equal, neither are they born free, but all in bonds to their ancestors and their environments. The success of government by the people will depend upon the stuff that people are made of. The people must guard, more jealously even than their liberties, the quality of their blood. A democracy like ours cannot afford to throw itself open to the world where every man is a lawmaker, every dull-witted or fanatical immigrant admitted to our citizenship is a bane to

---

★In fact, the term "melting pot" came into common use thanks to Israel Zangwill, whose 1908 play by that name attracted some attention at the time, including from Theodore Roosevelt, who attended its opening in Washington, D.C., in 1909. Says the hero of the play: "America is God's Crucible, the great Melting-Pot where all the races of Europe are melting and reforming . . . Germans and Frenchmen, Irishmen and Englishmen, Jews and Russians—into the Crucible with you all! God is making the American."

the commonwealth; where all classes of society merge insensibly into one another. Every alien immigrant or inferior race may bring corruption to the stock. There are races more or less akin to our own whom we may admit freely and get nothing but the infusion of their wholesome blood. But there are other races which we cannot assimilate without a lowering of our racial standard, which should be as sacred to us as the sanctity of our homes.

Political scientist Richard Ellis, author of *To the Flag: The Unlikely History of the Pledge of Allegiance,* argues that five anxieties loomed large "in the creation, propagation and amending of the Pledge of Allegiance": immigrants, materialism, freedom, radicals, communism.

The most compelling concern for Bellamy and his contemporaries were the new Americans, those people who were arriving by the boatload each day. Although we celebrate this as a country of immigrants, Ellis argues, that sentiment "exists side-by-side with fear and sometimes loathing." At almost the same time, 1883, Emma Lazarus composed her great sonnet for immigrants, a part of whose celebratory invitation was eventually attached to the base of the Statue of Liberty:

> *Give me your tired, your poor,*
> *Your huddled masses yearning to breathe free,*
> *The wretched refuse of your teeming shore.*
> *Send these, the homeless, tempest-tossed to me,*
> *I lift my lamp beside the golden door!*

It is no coincidence then that the Statue of Liberty in New York Harbor was dedicated in 1886, just a few years before the Public School Celebration of the continent's discovery and in the midst of an intense immigrant wave.

The Columbus Day celebration and the creation of the Pledge happened in the midst of an era that quite literally changed the complexion of America. The immigration anxiety continued, however, into the 1920s, when Bellamy's original words—"I pledge allegiance to my flag"—were changed to "I pledge allegiance to the flag of the United States of America" to ensure that immigrant children were not referring to the flag of their country of origin. The change was made to eliminate any confusion in the minds of those children, as well as to impart to them identification with their new country. Though the "my flag" problem may not have been foreseen by them, Bellamy and his *Companion* colleagues did anticipate the importance of instilling habits of national identity at an early age.

"Our school's [sic] great task," announced the *Companion,* was to make each child into a "thorough going American." And its editors had done their homework. They cited Census Bureau data showing that, in 1892, a third of all children in the country between the ages of five and seventeen had foreign-born parents or had themselves been born in another country. "It is the problem of our schools," concluded the *Companion,* "to assimilate these children to an American standard of life and ideas."

"The Pledge was a way of sending the patriotic message across America, bringing Columbus Day to the towns and the villages," says Marilyn Paul, a curator at the National Archives. "It was really a very grassroots idea."

Bellamy viewed the Columbus Day Celebration and the creation of the Pledge as a powerful moment for public education. The Pledge would, as Peter Dreier and Dick Flacks wrote in *The Nation* in 2002, "promote a moral vision to counter the individualism embodied in capitalism and expressed in the climate of the Gilded Age, with its robber barons and exploitation of workers. Bellamy intended the line 'One nation indivisible with liberty and justice for all' to express a more collective and egalitarian vision of America."

Bellamy held that the capitalist individualism of the late nineteenth century was inconsistent with Christianity, and like slavery before it, capitalism was destined to disappear, as well. But despite this strong belief in Christian socialism there is little in the pledge (or the Columbus Day celebration) that was overtly socialist.

Between his resignation from the pulpit (1889) and the Columbus Day Celebration (1892), Bellamy traded God for the new Americanism in his proselytizing. During that time, he joined the Lyceum League lecture circuit and addressed large influential groups speaking primarily about "Americanism in the Public Schools." Key speeches were made to the National Education Association (NEA) and the Women's Literary Union.

In the NEA speech on July 15, 1892, Bellamy credited Balch's salute (used in the New York City schools at the time) with having a positive effect on the immigrant children of that city. The salute, he said, made their new country real to these children, and the flag had the power to "Americanize" them.

Bellamy spoke at length about liberty, an American trait that had been "run into the ground," he said. The problem was not with liberty itself, he argued, but with liberty in the hands of corporate America, which he considered too greedy. Liberty for corporations was not, in Bellamy's view, "liberty and justice for all."

That was all well and good. It was when the former preacher began to talk about individual liberties that he drifted off into being what Richard Ellis called a "race conscious nativist."

"The hard, inescapable fact," as Bellamy had written, "is that men are not born equal." His opinion was not unique in America at the time; he was not alone in his apprehension about immigration.

But like Balch before him, Bellamy, while holding and expressing racist beliefs and ethnic prejudice, believed strongly in the transformative power of America and its institutions. He believed that America had the power to elevate peasants, former slaves, and common laborers. Enlightening the poor immigrant using rituals like the flag salute and the Pledge of Allegiance was imperative if the nation was going to maintain control of its ideals.

Though all the elements of the 1892 Columbus Day school celebration were quickly forgotten, except "The Bellamy Pledge," the event was nevertheless just the beginning of the organizers' vision of bringing a political socialization program to the public schools. As patriotic fervor in the country increased, the Pledge changed, and as it changed was steadily woven into the fabric of everyday life in America.

During the final decade of the nineteenth century, the flag was transformed into an important patriotic symbol in large part because of the Pledge and the *Youth's Companion* efforts to make the Columbus Day celebration a permanent presence in the lives of schoolchildren and adults. The intense emotional build-up before the Spanish American War brought about the informal custom of standing in the presence of the flag as it passed. Momentum continued to build for the school flag movement well into the last decade of the nineteenth century. Wisconsin was the first state to pass a law, in 1889, allowing school boards to purchase flags with public funds, but by 1900, just eleven years later, nineteen states and territories had made flying the flag over a school mandatory.

Just six months after the Columbus Day celebration, on April 25, 1893, James Upham and Francis Bellamy joined William McDowell to help celebrate the installation of his soaring flagpole on the coast of New Jersey. It was the first adult recitation of the Pledge at the National Liberty Pole and Flag Raising Ceremony at the Sandy Hook Navesink Lighthouse, the brightest light on the eastern seaboard, with a broad view of New York Harbor to the north.

* * *

The fact that both Upham and Bellamy attended the event was recognition of the role the *Youth's Companion* had played in the resurgent flag movement, and Upham was asked to give the key speech at the event. It was short, but had the mark of oratory that echoed the welcome optimism of Emma Lazarus:

> America has crossed the threshold of her supreme century. Preceding centuries have built but the framework of our nation. Shall America fulfill her divine mission? Then must she train leaders loyal only to right.
>
> The times demand a patriotic citizenship, patriotic schools, a patriotic pulpit, a patriotic press. Patriotism in its broadest sense is the propelling force behind this multitude of thoughtful, earnest young men, whose generous action makes this event today possible. . . .
>
> As the future shall behold them floating in their majestic mission, may all hearts wave a glad welcome to the coming millions; a welcome not in bondage and superstitions of the past, but to freedom, enlightenment and human brotherhood.

Bellamy was afforded the opportunity to lead the small group in the recitation of the Pledge as the huge flag waved, though the New York *Herald Tribune* incorrectly reported the words recited at the lighthouse as: "I vow myself to my flag and the Republic for which it stands, and liberty and justice for all."

In fact, not until after the turn of the century did the Bellamy pledge emerge from the pack and get recognition as *the* Pledge. The act of showing deference to the flag with a "salute" was by then deeply embedded in the national psyche. But the first flag salute statute was passed in New York State on the day after the United States declared war on Spain, April 22, 1898.

The bill was introduced in the state Senate by Senator Henry Coggeshall and required that the U.S. flag be flown ·over all public schools.

> It shall be the duty of the school authorities of every public school in the several cities and school districts of the State to purchase a United States flag, flagstaff and the necessary appliances therefor, and to display such flag upon or near the public school building during school hours, and at such other times as such school authorities may direct.

The law also directed the state superintendent of public instruction to prepare "a program for a salute to the flag at the opening of each day of school and such patriotic exercises as may be deemed by him to be expedient. . . ." Interestingly, in keeping with a theme stressed by many of the government officials Bellamy interviewed prior to the public school event in 1892, the New York legislators forbade using any of the flag ceremonies for military purposes:

> Nothing herein contained shall be construed to authorize military instruction or drill in the public schools during school hours.

The superintendent, Charles Rufus Skinner, a former editor of the Watertown *Daily Republican* and U.S. congressman, noted that the law said "not a word" about its intent. So he intended to provide one: "But whoever will read between the lines cannot fail to see its gracious purpose,—nothing less or other than to awaken in the minds and hearts of the young a strong and abiding regard for the flag and intelligent appreciation of the great men and great deeds that made it to be, to all American youth, the rallying-cry of patriotism."

Skinner got so carried away with the project that the "program" the law required turned into a huge 470-page *Manual of Patriotism*. "I would be glad to have every pupil in our public schools commit to memory each week some patriotic selection or quotation, no matter how brief it be," wrote Skinner in the preface. "Let school be opened by a patriotic song and a salute to the flag. This may be followed by a short recitation or by several brief patriotic quotations from the masterpieces which have been arranged in this work."

The tome was filled with dozens of poems, salutes, songs, and activities for use in the classroom and is a treasure trove for historians of the era who wish to find a single source for turn-of-the-century arcana of patriotism. It has, of course, things we recognize as standards—like "The Star-Spangled Banner" and "America"—but most of the content of this book has been lost from our collective memories. Like "The Flag That Has Never Known Defeat,"attributed to songwriters Charles L. Benjamin and George D. Sutton:

> On history's crimson pages, high up on the roll of fame
> The story of Old Glory burns, in deathless words of flame.
> 'Twas cradled in war's blinding smoke, amid the roar of guns,
> Its lullabies were battle-cries, the shouts of Freedom's sons;
> It is the old red, white, and blue, proved emblem of the free,
> It is the flag that floats above our land of liberty.
> Then greet it, when you meet it, boys, the flag that waves on high;
> And hats off, all along the line, when Freedom's flag goes by.

Chorus:

> Uncover when the flag goes by, boys,
> 'Tis freedom's starry banner that you greet,
> Flag famed in song and story,

Long may it wave, Old Glory,
The flag that has never known defeat.

All honor to the Stars and Stripes, our glory and our pride,
All honor to the flag for which our fathers fought and died;
On many a blood-stained battle-field, on many a gory sea,
The flag has triumphed, evermore triumphant may it be.
And since again, 'mid shot and shell, its folds must be unfurled,
God grant that we may keep it still unstained before the world,
All hail the flag we love, may it victorious ever fly,
And hats off, all along the line, when freedom's flag goes by.

Chorus:

Uncover when the flag goes by, boys, etc.

There are essays and interviews, including a conversation between one General Horry and a General (Francis) Marion, supposedly conducted in 1795 and titled "Free Schools Inspire Loyalty to Country." "Israel of old, you know, was destroyed for lack of knowledge," it begins; "and all nations, all individuals, have come to naught from the same cause. . . ." Many of the entries are quite good, even if their authors have disappeared into the fog of history, like this from one E. C. Cheverton:

Uncover to the flag; bare head
Sorts well with heart as, humbly bowed
We stand in presence of the dead
Who make the flag their shroud

Other entries are accompanied by names most of us know: Daniel Webster, reminiscing about "the towering marble of my country's Capitol"; or "Thou too, sail on, O ship of state! / Sail on, O Union, strong and great!" by Henry Wadsworth Longfellow.

The *Manual* also included examples of six different "patriotic pledges" that could be used for the flag salute at the start of each day. Bellamy's pledge was number five on the list and Balch's not mentioned at all:

No. 1.

Flag of Freedom! True to thee, All our Thoughts,
Words, Deeds shall be,—
Pledging steadfast Loyalty!

No. 2.

The toil of our Hands,
The thoughts of our Heads,
The love our Hearts,
We pledge to our Flag!

No. 3.

By the Memories of the Past,
By the Present, flying fast,
By the Future, long to last,
Let the dear Flag wave!

No. 4.

I pledge myself to stand by the flag that
stands for Loyalty, Liberty and Law!

Though Bellamy's Pledge (identified in the *Manual* as "The *Youth's Companion* 'Pledge of Allegiance'") was fifth, it was the only one to be accompanied by directions on how to salute the flag:

(Right hand lifted, palm downward to a line with
the forehead and close to it, standing thus, all repeat

together slowly:) "I pledge allegiance to my Flag and to the Republic for which it stands; One Nation indivisible, with Liberty and Justice for All." (At the words "to my Flag," the right hand is extended gracefully, palm upward towards the Flag and remains in this gesture to the end of the affirmation; whereupon all hands immediately drop to the side.)★

Others tried to take advantage of patriotism's popularity, but it was hard to compete with Skinner's massive state-sponsored *Manual.* The Woman's Relief Corps, for example, a strong promoter of the flag salute, attempted to distribute the American Flag Manufacturing Company's booklet "Ritual for Teaching Patriotism in the Public Schools," but as Ellis points out, schools were put off by the fact that the booklet carried advertising for the flag company and did not use it.

The Nation pounced on Skinner's tome for promoting "flag-fetishism" in a December 6, 1900, editorial. "Reading drivel to children and making them sing doggerel can hardly have any effect except to vulgarize them," said the magazine. "We believe that there is left enough of the old saving grace of humor to send this big and foolish book into the obscurity which yawns for the bathetic. What is really serious—and the only thing that warrants our giving it a moment's attention—is that it bears the imprimatur of the State Superintendent, and that it is to be inflicted upon our schools."

But it was not enough to stop the legions of patriots pushing for more flag appreciation. The Grand Army of the Republic

---

★A variation on the salute protocol was given in a 1912 book called *Flag Day: Its History, Origin, and Celebration as Related in Song and Story:* "1. Eyes on flag, right hand touching forehead, face uplifted: 'I pledge allegiance.' 2. Right arm waving outward and upward, palm up: 'To my flag and the country for which it stands, One nation, indivisible.' 3. Expansive gesture, both arms waving out. 'With liberty and justice.' 4. Hand brought down to side: 'for all.'"

officially endorsed the salute in 1899, and in 1905 its chief aide in charge of military instruction and patriotic education in schools, Allan Bakewell, circulated detailed instructions on a salute program in the group's August 1 newsletter. "The flag should be floated daily over every school-house," he said. "[A]nd, if any State has not yet on its statute books a law requiring this, all Aides in such States are urged to endeavor to secure such a law."

Bakewell continued:

> It should not be hoisted and lowered in a mere perfunctory way, but with ceremony and salutation. My recommendation to the National Encampment that there should be but one pledge in the salute met with favor, therefore the only pledge recommended is, "I pledge allegiance to my flag and to the republic for which it stands, one nation indivisible, with liberty and justice to all." This form of pledge, with instructions for saluting, will be furnished upon requisition.
>
> The Woman's Relief Corps, with whom you are urged to co-operate, are most earnest in this work of educating the youth to be patriotic, and you will find the Department President fully instructed by the National Patriotic Instructor and ready to join in every reasonable endeavor. . . .
>
> Let us all stand firmly together then, as if it were to be the last year in which we would have the privilege of serving our country. We must dispute the advance of anarchy. We must do all we can to prevent confusion by enrolling a large body in the interest of peace. Whoever shall be taught to respect the flag will always be ready to protect it. And, wherever it shall fly, it must be for the protection of the weak, a menace to inhumanity, a banner of good will and honor for all mankind.

Bakewell then explained again the proper etiquette in saluting the flag:

> At the given hour in the morning the pupils are assembled and in their places in the school. A signal is given by the principal of the school. Every student or pupil rises in his place. The flag is brought forward to the principal or teacher. While it is being brought forward from the door to the stand of the principal or teacher, every pupil gives the flag the military salute, which is as follows:—
>
> The right hand uplifted, palm upward, to a line with the forehead, close to it. While thus standing with the palm upward and in the attitude of salute, all the pupils repeat together, slowly and distinctly, the following pledge:—
>
> "I pledge allegiance to my Flag and to the Republic for which it stands: One Nation indivisible, with Liberty and Justice for All."
>
> At the words "to my Flag," each one extends the right hand gracefully, palm upward, toward the flag, until the end of the pledge of affirmation. Then all hands drop to the side. The pupils still standing, all sing together in unison the song "America,"—"My Country, 'tis of thee."
>
> In the primary departments, where the children are very small, they are taught to salute in silence, as an act of reverence, unaccompanied by any pledge. At a signal, as the flag reaches its station, the right hand is raised, palm downward, to a horizontal position against the forehead, and held there until the flag is dipped and returned to a vertical position. Then, at a second signal, the hand is dropped to the side,

and the pupil takes his seat. The silent salute con-
forms very closely to the military and naval salute to
the flag.

With America's entry into World War I in 1917, the demand
for flags hit an all-time high. Between April 1916 and May 1917,
the cost of flags increased 100 to 300 percent.

During that same time, Major League Baseball (like other
sports organizations) began the practice of playing "The Star-
Spangled Banner" at the beginning of every game in a gesture
of support for the military, and people stood. Within organizations like the Boy Scouts and Girl Scouts, the flag ritual became
a focal point.

By 1918 the adoration of the flag was such that commentators
began to describe the fixation in religious terms. In fact, that
year, William Norman Guthrie, a clergyman and lecturer in
literature at universities like the University of Chicago, published his *The Religion of Old Glory*. Guthrie "undertakes to interpret the historical meaning and the spiritual significance of
the American flag," said *The New York Times* at the time. "Our
national banner, he holds, conveys and inculcates lessons of patriotism and emblemizes what he calls 'the faith to which, as
Americans, we're born.' He considers separately and together the
flag's elements of form, color, design, and number, and from his
study draws the conviction that the flag is worthy of the reverence and worship of good Americans."

As more states adopted Uniform Flag laws, prosecutions for
desecrating or "insulting" the flag rose. It was in this context,
and the thick of war, that Congress passed the Espionage Act of
1917, which outlawed "insubordination, disloyalty, mutiny, refusal of duty, in the military or naval forces of the United
States" and the willful obstructing of "the recruiting or enlist-
ment service of the United States," and the Sedition Act of 1918,

which went further, and made it a violation of law to, among other things, "willfully utter, print, write or publish any disloyal, profane, scurrilous, or abusive language about the form of government of the United States or the Constitution of the United States, or the military or naval forces of the United States, or the flag of the United States, or the uniform of the Army or Navy of the United States. . . ." So it seemed not so odd that state flag statutes cracked down on desecrations: "No person shall publicly mutilate, deface, defile, defy, trample upon, or by word or act cast contempt upon any such flag, standard, color, ensign or shield."

In one case, E. V. Starr of Montana was sentenced to ten years behind bars when he refused to kiss the flag. Accounts of the time indicate that in March 1918, Starr was confronted by a group of people who attempted to convince him to kiss the flag. He refused, and said, "nothing but a piece of cotton with a little paint on it and some other marks in the corner there. I will not kiss that thing. It might be covered with microbes." This statement was believed to be seditious. He was charged and five months later, sentenced and fined.

In 1918, Congress went on to pass the Sabotage Act and the Sedition Act, criminalizing "any expression of opinion that was disloyal, profane or abusive of the American form of government, flag or uniform."

It was thus not extraordinary that the first mandatory flag salute law was passed in Washington State on March 13, 1919. It was a time of labor unrest in the Northwest. That January the city of Seattle was on the brink of a general strike after thirty-five thousand shipyard workers walked off the job and called for the rest of Seattle's workers to join them. The conflict raised fears of radical agitators and the possibility of a "homegrown socialist revolution." Calls for "revolution" by the striking workers evoked an emotional response, especially in light of the recent Russian Revolution.

Seattle's mayor, Ole Hansen, warned that the Industrial Workers of the World union, which was orchestrating the strike, was attempting "to take possession of our American Government and try[ing] to duplicate the anarchy of Russia."

The general strike fizzled due to public opinion, but the same day it ended the Washington State legislature passed the law that required schools to teach "the principles of American citizenship" and to prevent the hiring of any employee previously dismissed for being unpatriotic. The mandatory pledge law passed three days later with very little resistance or question. It held that school boards in Washington "shall cause appropriate flag exercises to be held in every school at least once in each week at which exercises the pupils shall recite the following salute to the flag: 'I pledge allegiance to my flag and the republic for which it stands, one nation indivisible, with liberty and justice for all.'"

The Washington law appears to be the first to direct that a specific salute be required, and that salute was to be Bellamy's Pledge of Allegiance. Failure to follow the law was a criminal misdemeanor.

Following passage of the Washington law, the Pledge became mandatory in schools beginning in the 1910s, until 1943, when the U.S. Supreme Court found the practice of forcing students to say the Pledge unconstitutional (*West Virginia State Board of Education v. Barnette*).

Following the end of World War I, the American Legion's National Americanism Commission—under the leadership of its director, Garland Powell—held two Flag Day conferences (over two years) and declared the U.S. flag "a living symbol of a living nation." The conferences brought together the major private sector patriotic organizations of the time. Members of the government were also present, including the secretary of education; President Warren Harding opened the conference.

"They are invading our homes, our schools, our churches,

and our very camps, our patriotic organizations, attacking our flag and our institutions," roared Mrs. Reuben Ross Holloway, national chairperson of the U.S. Daughters of 1812 and chair of Maryland's Correct Use of the Flag Committee. The "they" referred to were all the perceived critics of America and its institutions.

The commission's primary objective was to create and implement one code of rules for "how to honor and revere the American flag." The two-day meeting would produce rules for citizens to follow for the display, raising, lowering, saluting, and folding of flags and dispatched a seven-member committee— among them representatives from the American Legion SAR, DAR, Daughters of the Confederacy, PTA, and Boy Scouts—to draft the details. The committee was also assisted by members of the military.

The commission recommended that Bellamy's Pledge of Allegiance be the nation's official pledge. It did not specify the manner of the salute, but did amend Bellamy's original wording: "I pledge allegiance to my flag" became "I pledge allegiance to the flag of the United States."

Commission member Gridley Adams took credit for pushing the change. Adams defended that position years later, saying, "I did not like those words 'my flag,' believing that any alien or Hottentot could, and with all sincerity, pledge allegiance to whatever National emblem he held in his mind's eye. I wanted the Pledge of Allegiance to be specifically American."

Adams, a high-school dropout who claimed his great-great-grandfather was Nathan Hale's roommate at Yale, went on to become chairman of the National Flag Code Committee and founder of the United States Flag Foundation. Though his language may not sit well with Americans today, he was an effective, if eccentric, patriot, advising Emily Post on flag etiquette and once chastising Franklin Roosevelt for improper use of Old Glory in the Oval Office.

"Of all the Americans whose eyes grow bright and whose pulses quicken at the sight of the Stars and Stripes and the sound of 'The Star Spangled Banner,' none reacts to either patriotic stimulus more briskly than a retired advertising man named Gridley Adams, a chipper, outspoken, egocentric, and contentious old gentleman who for the better part of the last thirty years has carried on an impassioned, public love affair with the flag of the United States of America." So wrote E. J. Kahn in one of the more notable *New Yorker* opening sentences—in length, if nothing else—for a wonderfully titled profile of Mr. Adams called "Three Cheers for the Blue, White, and Red." Kahn was then writing, in July of 1952, in honor of the flag enthusiast's eighty-fifth birthday. And he painted the "advertising man" as a lovable oddball who was pretty much a one-man show on the flag decorum scene. As it turned out, both the Flag Code Committee and the Flag Foundation were headquartered, according to Kahn, in "a four-room apartment Adams and his eighty-year-old wife, whom he married in 1898, occupy in Peter Cooper Village in New York City."

Regardless of his quirks, Adams had an impact on the nation's attitude toward its flag. And during the Americanism Commission's second conference in 1924, the "to my flag" line was amended again, at Gridley's insistence, to read, "I pledge allegiance to the flag of the United States of America."

"[P]eople ought to be sure which United States they're talking about," Adams said in defense of the change.

Bellamy, then almost seventy but closely following the discussions from his retirement home in Tampa, Florida, disliked the changes—they were "needless," he said, and "interrupt the rhythm and make the Pledge harder to say." A wordsmith to the end, Bellamy had left *Youth's Companion* in 1895, finding it hard to have any assignments matching the excitement of the Public School Celebration. After a four-month stint with *Ladies' Home Journal,* the former minister settled in with *The Illustrated American* as an editor. Unfortunately, without the moderating influence of an uplifting goal—unifying America through a celebration of the flag—Bellamy fell under the sway of some of his darker tendencies. In an 1897 editorial for the magazine he wrote the line about men "not born equal." This was the launching pad for his advice about the country being on guard against certain immigrants; not the "races, more or less akin to our own," he had said, but the "other races which we cannot assimilate without a lowering of our racial standard."

When *The Illustrated American* was sold in 1898, Bellamy went to work for a book publisher (where he edited and published his cousin Edward's last, posthumous book, *The Duke of Stockbridge*), then did some reporting for the *New York Sun,* then some writing for the Equitable Life Assurance Society.

He finally landed a job at *Everybody's Magazine,* where he would stay for eleven years. And though *Everybody's* had a muckraking reputation, with Lincoln Steffens on its editorial board, Bellamy stayed out of trouble, working as an advertising manager. Even at that, however, he found an "audience," writing a well-received book called *Effective Magazine Advertising.* This landed him a job as an account executive at a New York advertising agency, where he stayed until his "semiretirement" in 1921. His wife Hattie had died in 1918 and in 1920 he married Marie Morin, with whom he moved to Tampa in 1922— and from where he would monitor the debate over his Pledge until his death in 1931 at age seventy-six.

Given his apparent lifelong fear of inferior races and places, one would have thought that Bellamy would welcome Gridley Adams's 1924 concern about the "my flag" part of his Pledge. But pride of authorship prevented Bellamy from accepting the change. In any case, his objections were ignored—in large part, no doubt, because this was exactly the period that his authorship of the Pledge was being challenged (see Chapter 7)—and the American Legion's Commission moved on to its other significant piece of work, during its second meeting that year: formalizing the salute. The group decided on one that was, essentially, a slight modification of what the Grand Army of the Republic had been suggesting for years: civilians were to stand with their "right hand over their heart," as the Pledge was recited. At the words "to the flag," the right hand was to be "extended, palm upward, toward the flag." A member of the military, in uniform, was to use the standard, right-hand salute while reciting the Pledge.

A permanent National Flag Code Committee was also formed at that meeting and Adams was made its chairman, but as Kahn would point out, the committee never met again:

> Those listed on his Flag Foundation stationery include General Douglas MacArthur (Honorary Chairman); Sergeant Alvin C. York (National Chairman); James A. Farley, William Green, and Gene Tunney (among a twenty-two-man advisory committee); and the Honorable Herbert Hoover, Captain E. V. Rickenbacker, the Honorable Harold R. Medina, General Lucius D. Clay, General William J. Donovan, Governor Thomas E. Dewey, Gilbert Grosvener, and George E. Sokolsky (among thirty-seven members-at-large). Adams got them all to serve by writing to them, but he has never called a meeting of the Foundation in its six years of existence, and is unacquainted with the majority of its sponsors.

Following the 1924 conference, the flag code was published in the Boy Scout handbook. The American Legion distributed six million pamphlets on flag etiquette to schools, churches, and public officials nationwide. A total of fourteen million pamphlets were distributed across the country.

In 1925, the Ku Klux Klan (with a membership of four million) endorsed the Flag Code and regularly instructed its younger members on flag etiquette. Prospective members swore an oath of allegiance to the flag and the U.S. Constitution, and they made a strong, clear link between religion and flag devotion. At its peak (in the mid-1920s), the Klan readily used the flag as part of its ritual. And on August 9, 1925, forty thousand hooded KKK members walked down Pennsylvania Avenue in Washington, D.C., holding thousands of American flags aloft. Aside from some of the more visible flag-burning incidents during the 1960s, this march remains one of the most visible reminders of the perils of elevating the flag to hyper-symbolic status.

" 'Shoot, if you must, this old gray head,' " went the lines of John Greenleaf Whittier's famous 1864 poem, " 'But spare your country's flag,' she said."

A heated debate arose during the 1930s over the salute's resemblance to that of the Nazis', both the DAR and the U.S. Flag Association reacted poorly, dismissing the concerns. The Pledge had become such an important piece of American life, such a potent symbol of nationalism, that it could not be allowed to be tainted by the Fascist association.

The American Legion and the Veterans of Foreign Wars (VFW) successfully saw the Flag Code passed into law. On June 22, 1942, the U.S. Flag Code became the law of the land. A joint resolution passed by Congress made the code Public Law 829 (Chapter 806, 77th Congress, 2nd session). The law sets out the rules for use and display of the flag, conduct during the playing of the national anthem, and the words of the Pledge of Allegiance to the Flag (Bellamy's) to be recited. The flag code also contained the raised-arm salute (as prescribed during the 1924 Flag Day conference). And despite the controversy among the general public, there was no discussion about the appropriateness of that salute within Congress.

With this act, the federal government had finally made the Pledge of Allegiance an official U.S. slogan, and guaranteed its part in the mainstream of American life. But was it Bellamy's Pledge?

7. WHO WROTE IT?

One day in early July 1923, Francis Bellamy was walking down Fifth Avenue in New York City. He had felt agitated for several months because his authorship of the Pledge of Allegiance, which had been written some thirty years before, was being disputed—again. This time he had heard it in a radio interview with the current owner of the *Youth's Companion* magazine. Bellamy had been passive in responding to previous challenges. But now, at age sixty-eight, he was ready to fight back.

The magazine had asserted that Bellamy's boss, James Upham, had actually drafted the Pledge in 1892, and then sent it down to the editorial staff for polishing. Perhaps it was the other way around. But the *Companion*'s statement dismissed Bellamy as just one of several junior editors who had a hand in wordsmithing the salute. While the statement acknowledged that the "name of Francis Bellamy of Massachusetts is sometimes associated with the Pledge," so was "Frank E. Bellamy, a Kansas schoolboy." Regardless, the magazine stated it was Mr. James B. Upham who had crafted the piece, and it was he who should be credited.

Bellamy commenced a vigorous defense of his authorship. He wrote a letter on June 19, 1923, to *Companion* owner C. E. Kelsey in which he asserted politely but firmly that he, Francis Bellamy, had written "every one of the 23 words . . . without the change of a single word by Mr. Upham or anyone else." Kelsey's eventual reply provided no satisfaction. Bellamy proceeded to pursue other sources that would corroborate his position.

It was quite by accident that Bellamy encountered Mr. and

Mrs. John Winfield Scott on that busy New York street in 1923. Scott had been in charge of the advertising office of the *Companion* during the time the Pledge was written. Both he and his wife, Florence, had participated in planning the national celebration during which the Pledge was first recited. They had also attended a first anniversary event in New York City. Both Upham and Bellamy had been present. The Scotts and Bellamy hadn't seen each other since. But when Bellamy disclosed the *Companion's* authorship challenge, the Scotts shared his outrage.

A few days later, on Bellamy's urging, Florence Scott wrote a detailed account of "our last meeting, about thirty years ago," that she had remembered for Bellamy at their Fifth Avenue encounter. It was at the ceremony raising the flag at the Navesink Highlands in New Jersey. And though her memory of the date was off by several months—"it was not before July 1893," she wrote—the rest of her account about the April event was extremely detailed, including a listing of the various attending dignitaries. She then recalled that Mr. Upham himself had introduced Bellamy as the writer of the Pledge. "It so happened that I was with Mr. Upham most of the day," she wrote, and "Mr. Upham introduced you to several other persons, as he did to me, as the writer of the Pledge of Allegiance. . . ." Finally, she described "the very climax of the proceedings . . . when you, as the author of the Pledge, were called upon to lead us in repeating it."

If the Pledge were written and published in a national journal today, there would be little doubt about who wrote it. The author's name would most certainly be shown. Take *Time* or *Newsweek,* the *New Yorker* or the *Atlantic Monthly,* even publications directed to the adolescent market, like *National Geographic Kids.* These magazines all identify the staff writers and others who contribute reports or collaborate on stories. None omits bylines or attribution, except for certain recurring features.

Not so with the *Youth's Companion.* It was the policy of the magazine, at least during Daniel Ford's ownership and Francis Bellamy's tenure, that the name of an employee who is an editorial contributor not be printed. This was an acknowledged rule, even though there is no evidence that it was written down anywhere. The message to salaried employees was: you work for and should promote the *magazine*; you should not seek to gain individual recognition or personal credit for your efforts.

Thus, when the Pledge was first printed in the "official programme" of the 1892 Columbus Day celebration, it was identified as the "*Youth's Companion* Pledge of Allegiance." Bellamy understood and accepted the nonattribution policy, though he later expressed objection to being denied signing rights. His superiors also felt that the new salute would be better received if it appeared "to emanate" from the national organization of public school superintendents that was sponsoring the event, rather than the hand of an individual.

Moreover, the Pledge had been conceived as a one-event exercise. It was written for the purpose of commemorating the four hundredth anniversary of America's discovery by Christopher Columbus. Its recitation would accompany President Benjamin Harrison's proclamation of the 1892 Columbus Day as a national holiday. It was not commissioned for flag-raising rituals or patriotic expressions going forward.

Bellamy was content with his work at the magazine and was stimulated by the national endeavor in which he was involved. He respected the publisher, Daniel Ford, and no doubt found him to be the "modest and self-effacing editor" that others described. (Ford's name did not even appear in the magazine until after his death in 1899; this also helps to explain the no-attribution policy.) Bellamy appreciated that "Mr. Ford selected me to aid [the] patriotic work of putting the Flag over the Schools." He was also proud of the "great opportunity" to chair the NEA executive committee. As for his immediate supervisor, James

Upham, who was related by marriage to Ford, Bellamy said he always enjoyed a collegial relationship.

When Bellamy left the *Companion* at the end of 1895, he made no public effort "to attach his name to the Pledge as the author." A "spirit of loyalty" prevented him from doing so, he said. But it was not long thereafter that the first challenge was mounted.

The challenge came from a grade-school student from Cherryvale, Kansas, a small town in the southeast corner of the state. His name was Frank Bellamy, but he was not related. Frank submitted the Pledge as his entry in a school contest in 1896. Apparently, the Columbus Day celebration of 1892 (four years previous) had not been remembered by the Cherryvale contest organizers because Frank won. He gained some local repute, and confused some national media. But Frank's fraud was quickly revealed, and Francis did not take much notice.

Francis Bellamy did notice an article that was published in the *Companion* on December 20, 1917. It was offered in response to an inquiry from Herbert Fison, the Malden, Massachusetts, librarian, asking who had written the Pledge. The editor's reply carried a story by staff member Seth Mendell and a photo of James B. Upham. The magazine's official view of the creation and authorship of the Pledge was unequivocal: "Mr. Upham had already written a form of the Pledge very much like that which is now so well known, and with the help of other members of the firm and of members of the editorial staff the present and final form was written."

Bellamy was astonished. And he became more so when the story was followed by a pamphlet affirming this claim was sent to libraries across the country. The pamphlet, which was also distributed to anyone who wrote to the magazine asking for clarification on authorship, clearly attributed the full creation of the pledge to Upham:

> Various patriotic men . . . have been mentioned as
> the authors, but there is no evidence to show that
> they did more than discuss and approve the rough
> draft prepared by Mr. Upham, and afterwards con-
> densed and perfected by him and his associates of the
> Companion force.

A written debate between Bellamy and the *Companion* en-
sued.

The author's challenge to his former employer became pro-
gressively heated. Imposed anonymity might be okay; acquiescence to credit given to someone else was not. Though it could
not offer substantiated evidence to the contrary, the magazine
refused to deal with Bellamy's claim and recant its attribution to
Upham.

Emotions simmered for several years—until reignited by a radio interview in 1923. In a series of written exchanges that summer, the *Companion*'s editor advised Bellamy that "the best course
seems to be to leave the matter where it stands: that is, that the
Pledge is the *Companion*'s Pledge, that the inspiration came from
Mr. Upham . . . and that no individual credit be given for work
done in carrying out any part of the general scheme."

Bellamy found this response to be not only obstinate, but he
labeled it maligning, dishonest, and hypocritical. Here was the
magazine crediting a man who had been dead for eighteen
years with something he had not accomplished, and then refused to correct the error because no credit to an individual
should be given! "Absurd!" Bellamy could not contain himself.
The *Companion*'s position was "grievously unjust," a "palpable
discourtesy," and "a collusion to suppress the truth." The publication refused to arbitrate further, and ceased responding to
Bellamy's letters after writing to Bellamy with one final heated
letter:

*Your third letter in regard to the Companion Pledge of
Allegiance does nothing to change our convictions. We
repeat that Mr. Mendell's account of the origin of the
Pledge was prepared with deliberate care soon after the
event and that Mr. Mendell was a man beyond most men,
exact and scrupulous in statement. We add that your
intimation that Mr. Mendell was actuated by any "malig-
nity" towards you to make a "dishonest" report of the
facts is preposterous. Against the careful statement of this
honorable man, you bring only your own unsupported and
interested assertions. We believe Mr. Mendell's account
implicitly.*

Bellamy died six years later, in 1931, at the age of seventy-six,
in Tampa. Despite the firm brush-off by the *Companion,* he
maintained his claim of authorship and repeated it to anyone
who would listen. In a speech shortly before his death he said: "I
have the happiness of realizing that I once, in my young man-
hood, contributed to my Country an easily remembered symbol
of patriotism which has become historic and has been in many
millions of individuals a spur to their love of Country and Flag."

He was buried in his hometown of Rome, New York, with-
out the acknowledgment he so desperately sought from the
Companion. But since the magazine closed its doors in 1929,
Bellamy at least enjoyed the satisfaction of outliving it. And
though he couldn't take pleasure in it, his friends and relatives
must have been content to read the obituary headline in *The
New York Times* on August 31, 1931: *FRANCIS M. BELLAMY,
PATRIOTIC WRITER, DIES; Author of "The Pledge to the
Flag" Is Stricken in Florida at the Age of 75.*★

★The *Times* not only got Bellamy's middle initial wrong—it is "J" for Julius—but
also his age; he was seventy-six.

The Upham Family Association of Malden, Massachusetts, a genealogical organization that included James Upham among descendants of the Upham clan in America, continued to press the issue of authorship to declare their family member the official author of the Pledge. And in 1930 the president of the U.S. Flag Association, Colonel James A. Moss, U.S. Army retired, approved the Upham claim based on the claims and evidence presented by the Upham family.

In 1936 the controversy resurfaced when it piqued the interest of a young woman from Portsmouth, Virginia. Twenty-two-year-old Margarette Miller, a self-described "wallflower type," was deeply moved by the recitation of the Pledge on Armistice Day (which is observed today on November 11 as Veterans Day). She soon threw herself into the mission of solving the conflicts of the Pledge's authorship.

Miss Miller (she never did marry) dispensed quickly with the lingering claim of Frank Bellamy, the Kansas schoolboy. She then moved on to James Upham, whom she discovered had descended from the original settlers of the Massachusetts Bay Colony. She embraced him as the author. She even persuaded her hometown newspaper, the *Portsmouth Star,* to salute Upham with a headline edition on his birthday.

Further, the Order of Job's Daughters of Portsmouth started plans to erect a $30,000 memorial to James Upham in Washington, D.C. Job's Daughters, a Masonic youth organization for girls aged thirteen to twenty, described themselves at the time with a goal to "band together girls for spiritual and moral upbringing, to teach love of country and flag . . . home, parents and elders."

Soon enough, however, Miller found herself confronted with a letter from David Bellamy of Rochester, New York. This was Francis's son. He told her that she was wrong about Upham, and that he remembered clearly his father writing the Pledge.

Miller sought a higher authority before the Job's Daughters memorial could be built. She went back to Colonel Moss at the

U.S. Flag Association to get him to restate in unqualified terms the Upham claim. Now questioned in this manner, Moss gave the matter an official bearing by having the association appoint a committee of three renowned academic historians—department heads from Fordham, Georgetown, and Washington universities—to review all available documents and render a definitive decision. They concluded in 1939 that it was in fact Francis Bellamy who wrote the Pledge and Colonel Moss reversed his previous declaration. *Time* magazine, reporting on Colonel Moss's reversal, said: "Caution probably cost Patriot Upham a sumptuous monument. Last week Colonel Moss penitently announced that Francis Bellamy wrote The Pledge."

Margarette Miller, who would go on to refer to herself as Dr. Miller after she was given an honorary doctorate from Upper Iowa University for her efforts in clarifying the Pledge authorship issue, chronicled her quest in a 1946 book entitled *Twenty-Three Words*.★

The authorship battle didn't end there, however. The U.S. Flag Association's conclusion came under renewed attack in the mid-1950s. The Upham Family Association again gathered evidence they said proved the case for James Upham. They revived the claim with help from David Brickman, editor, and Archie Birtwell, staff reporter, of the *Malden Evening News*.

In a series of five articles, Birtwell presented the Upham case in a step-by-step recounting of the story and the evidence he uncovered. Part of the documented proof that the Upham family gathered (and which Birtwell used in his articles) were sworn affidavits from members of the staff of the *Companion* who were working at the publication at the time of the drafting of the

---

★The book is packed with documents, but the problem was its subtitle: *The Life Story of the Author of the Pledge of Allegiance as Told in His Own Words*. This was odd since there is no evidence that Miller ever met Bellamy. Adding to the problem, Miller's research papers were given to an upstate New York businessman who has so far refused to share them with researchers.

Pledge. The affidavits were emphatic in favor of the Upham claim, if not precise with the details. One former staff member said: "I can recall his [Upham] reading it and explaining it to me, and his enthusiasm concerning it as combined with the flag-on-every-schoolhouse campaign." Another staff member, a former editor who was close to Upham, was more specific: "Mr. Upham wrote it; it was handed to each of the editors and partners in turn for comment, criticism and suggestion." Another former editor echoed this memory: "The idea and the original draft of the Flag Pledge came from Mr. James B. Upham. . . . some minor polishing was contributed by other members of the Companion Group. . . . All those who have knowledge of the matter insist emphatically that it is highly erroneous to describe anyone except Mr. James B. Upham as the 'author' of the Pledge."

The *Evening News* series also repeated the details of a face-to-face interview between an Upham family member and Francis Bellamy that was conducted in Tampa and used to get the nod for the Upham claim from the U.S. Flag Association in 1930. During the interview, the Upham representative pressed Bellamy for copies of any original notes or proofs of the Pledge from the time when it was written. Bellamy had nothing. In fact, as the Upham supporters were quick to point out, Bellamy had no evidentiary materials relating to the Pledge until after Upham's death in 1905. A Tampa lawyer who witnessed the 1929 exchange would later write: "From the result of the interview I became thoroughly convinced that Mr. Bellamy was not the author of the 'Pledge to the Flag.' His conduct was that of a gentleman throughout during the interview, but somewhat theatrical, and I formed the distinct impression that he was a lover of publicity and not opposed to seeking it when the occasion was presented."

With such a direct assault on the Bellamy claim, the Bellamy family countered with David Bellamy issuing a public request through a 1956 letter to the *Christian Science Monitor* that the controversy be elevated to a still-higher authority—the Library of Congress. "The issue should be settled soberly and calmly by a study of the prima-facie evidence on both sides," he wrote.

The Library of Congress accepted the appeal. A further, even more exhaustive study was undertaken. After a year and a half of work, a thirty-five-thousand-word report was issued with the following conclusion:

> Unless one is prepared to believe that Francis Bellamy was a deliberate and conscienceless liar, the mass of his testimony is overwhelmingly in his favor.
>
> We, for our part, do not believe that Francis Bellamy did lie. . . . We are therefore constrained to pronounce in his favor.

Congressman Kenneth Keating (R.-N.Y.) delivered the document to Congress on August 8, 1957, saying that he "hoped that this definitive report will end once and for all any dispute as to the pledge's authorship."

The Upham family would never again directly challenge the actual authorship attribution. But the group, now called the Upham Family Society, Inc., with its membership headquarters in the 1703 Upham home and family homestead in Melrose, Massachusetts, continues to maintain that without Upham there would be no Pledge. At the minimum, an Upham Family Society spokesperson says, Upham "wrote something like 'I pledge allegiance to my flag and to the Republic for which it stands' and turned the matter over to Francis Bellamy and maybe a whole committee." And while the organization has put the issue to rest as far as the Library of Congress determination of official authorship, the membership card of the Upham Family Society reads in part: "Pledge originated by James Bailey Upham, Malden, MA."

8. THE COURTS
AND THE CONSTITUTION

While the battle over authorship kept the Bellamy and Upham camps busy for decades, another set of conflicts over the Pledge raged with greater and greater intensity. They were not about wording or authorship, but about the use of the Pledge as a universal American expression of national loyalty and whether you could force people to say it. Detractors of the Pledge insisted that one aspect or another of what had become an unofficial national oath contradicted the Pledge's promise of "liberty and justice for all." Mandatory recitations, quickly common in schools and town halls throughout the land, according to these critics, violated freedoms guaranteed by the Constitution of the very Republic for which the flag stood. So far, and some scholars don't think we're done, legal challenges to the Pledge have taken our national oath to the U.S. Supreme Court three different times.

An ever-present backdrop to all the legal fights is the Pledge's overwhelming and broad-based support and acceptance by Americans. In virtually every poll of adults conducted over the years, the oath gets almost universal approval. No matter how the question is posed, between 80 and 95 percent of Americans consistently judge the Pledge perfect. The wording is perfect. The manner in which it is observed is perfect. The loyalty promises expressed when saying the Pledge are perfect. The emphasis on instructing schoolchildren in universal patriotism through the ceremony of the Pledge is perfect. The legal requirement in many states to recite the Pledge is perfect.

But, this being America, the minority, however small, has rights. And it can express them. And no matter how "perfect" the Pledge and how large the majority that supports it, its very existence calls attention to one of the basic freedoms of Americans: the freedom to opt out, to dissent. The widespread approval for the Pledge is not lost on politicians who frequently "wrap themselves in the flag" to prove their patriotism. Nor is it lost on the judges who have had to weigh the often sticky issues raised by legal challenges to the Pledge against the will of such a large percentage of Americans who don't want to see it tampered with.

Still, even though faced with such large popular odds against them, the critics of the Pledge, drawn from a wide spectrum of perspectives, from the deeply religious to atheists and from civil rights activists to pacifists, have been persistent in their belief that forced recitation of the Pledge compromises basic rights of freedom of choice—both political and religious—that the flag is supposed to represent.

New York State started this part of the argument in 1898, when it became the first state to pass a law calling for statewide adoption of a Pledge to be used in the schools.

Over the next twenty years, several states copied the New York statute and passed their own flag salute laws, including Washington State, the first to mandate the recitation of the Pledge "at least once in each week."

In the next few years, as more and more states passed similar statutes—and as more and more local communities passed laws governing the use of the Pledge in those states that did not have statewide statutes—the mandatory nature of the laws became more and more punitive. In most cases they penalized teachers— usually by dismissal—for not leading their students in reciting the Pledge. Presumably, the state legislators thought students would automatically follow the mandatory lead of the teachers; they did not anticipate students refusing. Thus, many local school districts expanded on the mandatory requirement by adopting punishment of students who either failed to recite the Pledge or who refused to.

The common punishment for students was expulsion from school until they agreed to return with the promise to recite the Pledge. Then, by 1918, some local communities started declaring and enforcing punishment for the parents of students who refused to recite the Pledge, including fines and/or imprisonment.

And this is when local controversies developed into a national debate that ultimately spiraled into unexpectedly violent and tragic consequences.

As often happens in a democracy, especially one as unfettered and decentralized as the United States was in the late nineteenth and early twentieth centuries, the Pledge laws came about as popular, almost spontaneous, local expressions and were generally enacted as a patriotic response to some historic event or social movement or political fear of the time. The 1898 New York State statute, for example, was enacted as a display of patriotic solidarity the day after the United States declared war on Spain. One hundred and three years later, following the September 11, 2001, terrorist attacks on the World Trade Center and the Pentagon, nearly a dozen states that previously did not have Pledge statutes passed them, bringing to forty-six the number of states with laws on reciting the Pledge.

Also, in the early part of the twentieth century, beginning in 1919 and throughout the 1920s and 1930s, there was a general concern about the effects of the Bolshevik Revolution in Russia and the growing incidents of radical political activity in the United States. As minor cracks in the concept of "indivisible" were noticed, there were increasing calls for public displays of loyalty that activities like the Pledge provided. And state and local laws followed.

But the personal convictions of some people found an untenable conflict with those laws. And no matter how popular mandatory recitation laws were, an increasing number of people saw them as stepping on the toes of their constitutional rights of freedom of personal choice and action—and used the principles that the Pledge espoused to fight its mandatory use. Only in America!

Although the use of the Pledge, and the laws that required it, grew fairly rapidly, there are few recorded incidents of protest against the Pledge until 1912. The deficit could be attributed to the fact that there wasn't any dissent or, more likely, news of any such protest was considered so minor that no one paid much attention. Considering the fact that what we today consider obvious violations of the First Amendment guarantees of free speech and press went almost unnoticed until the 1920s (the American Civil Liberties Union was formed in 1920 in large part to rectify this oversight), it is surely not a historical stretch to think that objections to the Pledge were both few and far between—and unremarked upon—for quite some time after its use became widespread.

Oddly enough, the earliest recorded incidents of protests—almost all of which involved schoolchildren who were required by state or local law to recite the Pledge—concerned foreign nationals who, although they resided in the United States and attended American public schools, still felt loyalty to their native flag of citizenship. To pledge allegiance to the symbol of the United States would, they argued, force them to, in effect, renounce a flag and country with which they felt greater alliance. And, in fact, swearing allegiance to a "foreign" flag would make them traitors to their own countries.

Though this may sound positively traitorous today—and it would sound even more so as soon as the United States entered World War I—it should be noted, again, that historic context suggests otherwise. Despite healthy nationalistic beliefs—the cause of countless wars—laws and customs relating to citizenship and patriotism have not always been so, well, nationalistic.

The Romans were thought to have invented the notion of formal citizenship as a way to legitimize their empire-building. And birth in a country has long been considered to automatically impart citizenship. But "citizenship" and "patriotism" didn't mean much except in times of empire-building, war, or for purposes of taxation in the dividing and redividing that had characterized European history.

The history of loyalties within the United States is something unique. We expect loyalty to the United States as a whole; to the individual State of birth or adoption; and, of course, to the individual and his or her "inalienable rights." There are also regional loyalties, which at the time of the Pledge's creation remained intense in the decades following the end of the Civil War. Southern states and local communities of the former Confederacy did not join in on the early push for mandatory Pledge participation with the same enthusiasm as their Northern counterparts, perhaps in an unstated ambivalence about requiring allegiance to a nation that Southern sentiment continued to question for years after the end of the Civil War.

The notion of national loyalty for loyalty's sake, the patriotic "my country right or wrong," is at the heart of the mandatory Pledge of Allegiance laws and a relatively new, at least inconsistently enforced, phenomenon. Europeans, for example, didn't need passports until World War I. The United States, of course, was created by "foreigners," and so had to invent forms of citizenship and nationalism as it went. Various American states and localities often created their own "passports" at different times in our history and for different reasons. And, as we have seen, "Americanism," as Francis Bellamy told the National Education Association in 1892, was a significant part of what the country needed to define. But though Bellamy was able to capture Americans' urge to unity, it was still very much an urge-aborning.

Still, the United States, despite trends and popular sentiment to the contrary, remains deeply suspicious, if ambivalent, about forced allegiances. To this day, for instance, the United States allows "dual citizenship." And the U.S. Supreme Court, as late as 1952 (*Kawakita v. United States*), ruled that dual citizenship is a "status long recognized in the law" and that "a person may have and exercise rights of nationality in two countries and be subject to the responsibilities of both. The mere fact he asserts the rights of one citizenship does not without more mean that he renounces the other."

Even if this were the official belief, it's not one that was exercised on the ground where most Americans live—and still live. Thus, initial reactions to refusals to recite the Pledge were often handled harshly by officials of local communities. During one such incident in New Jersey in 1912, for instance, a student who refused to say the Pledge was expelled with an admonition from a school board member that the student:

> should go to a private school and pay for his tuition
> or go back to Canada or England. But if we make an
> exception in his favor I suppose that any anarchist
> might refuse to salute the flag.

Indeed, while this school board member expressed a sense of an implied threat from an "anarchist" when a non-U.S. citizen objected to reciting the Pledge, another New Jersey community during the same year had to contend with the objections of a self-professed political "radical." In this situation a boy refused to participate in the Pledge ceremony because he claimed that his parents were Socialists who only held allegiance to the "Red flag." And while political objections of this sort arose, other perspectives offered a different set of objections. In 1916, for example, a black elementary-school student in Chicago refused to Pledge to the flag because the flag represented to him a country purposely oppressive toward black people and not representing the "liberty and justice for all" that the Pledge celebrated.

In each of these early incidents, the local officials, after much huffing and puffing that included expelling the students from school—and in the case of the Chicago student, arrest and trial—the students were quietly let back into school and not forced to participate in the Pledge.

The next wave of challenges would be more serious and prove to be the source of the legal battles that would ultimately take the question of mandatory pledging to the U.S. Supreme Court. These challenges would be based primarily on religious grounds. The first major religious opposition to the Pledge came from the Mennonites, an Anabaptist and generally conservative religious sect that was also adamantly antiwar in all forms. And in 1918, as the United States was entering World War I, the group found in the Pledge a perfect symbol with which to express their pacifist beliefs. (The Amish, or Amish Mennonites, are a separate sect, having broken from the Mennonites in the late seventeenth century. Amish and Mennonite communities, however, are often found clustered together geographically throughout the world.)

The Mennonite objection to the Pledge in 1918 was summarized by one of the sect's leaders:

> Pledging allegiance to a flag as we see it, though we honor and respect it, at least implies a Pledge to defend it against all its enemies, which would mean to resort to arms and to take human life.

One of the first tests of the Mennonite position came in 1918 when a Mennonite father in Ohio was prosecuted, convicted, and sentenced to a twenty-five-day jail term because he had told his nine-year-old daughter not to recite the Pledge at school. The child was sent home each day she refused to say the Pledge and the father was convicted of allowing his child to be truant from school. The father, in appealing this conviction, argued that he did not keep his child home from school but had, in fact, sent her to school every day. It was, he claimed, the school that had sent her home.

The appeals court took the side of the lower court, concluding that if the father had not told the child to refuse to say the Pledge, she would not have been sent home and, therefore, it was the father's fault the child was truant. The court also offered a stern lecture on the patriotic importance of reciting the Pledge:

> Such conduct on the part of our citizens is not conscionable, for conscience would lead to respect for government and to its defense, especially in time of war, but rather it is the forerunner of disloyalty and treason.

For decades, similar court rulings prevailed over comparable religious objections to the Pledge. But none of these cases reached a boiling point of national attention. This was due in large part to the fact that nearly all of these early cases were settled quietly and on a local level. Often the conflict was resolved simply by allowing the student to delay coming to school until after the morning Pledge ceremony was performed.

During the 1920s, however, groups on both sides of the issue—one demanding universal mandatory adherence to reciting the Pledge, the other demanding voluntary involvement that permitted abstention from the ceremony when it compromised personal convictions—began polarizing in stronger and stronger ways.

On the Pledge support side, groups such as the American Legion, the VFW, and the DAR lobbied successfully to broaden and strengthen state statutes requiring the Pledge. They also pushed to force local communities to enforce the statutes. These efforts picked up speed and intensity following the National Flag Conferences of 1923 and 1924—at the same time that Francis

Bellamy was beginning to defend his authorship of the Pledge. These conferences, sponsored by the United States Flag Association, provided the first "official" nationwide guidelines for proper flag etiquette—although it wouldn't be until 1942 that the federal government would adopt truly official guidelines—and would galvanize supporters of the Pledge.

On the other side of the issue, the American Civil Liberties Union (ACLU), formed to defend First Amendment rights, took up the issue as a cause. And though Pledge opponents weren't as well organized or well funded as those supporting the Pledge, in the early 1930s one religious group emerged with the resolve—and, more importantly, the resources—to ultimately bring the issue to a head in the U.S. Supreme Court: Jehovah's Witnesses.

The Jehovah's Witnesses, a Christian sect that today has a worldwide membership of some seven million followers, was founded in the late nineteenth century as the Zion's Watch Tower Tract Society. Changing its name to Jehovah's Witnesses in 1931, the group may seem an unlikely champion of First Amendment rights. But the fervently evangelical antiestablishment group had already been the object of mob violence for its contentious views on Catholics. Its "unpatriotic" beliefs included simple spurning of political involvement to pacifist opposition to military service. During the height of World War I, in May 1918, the president and board of directors of the Witnesses were indicted by the U.S. government for violating the Espionage Act. The indictment accused the heads of the group with conspiring to cause disloyalty to the United States and refusal of military duty. They were found guilty and sentenced to twenty years' imprisonment. However, in March 1919, the judgment against them was reversed, and they were released from prison and the charges later dropped.

Still, these were long odds for a small religious group that was uncompromising in its positions against a force as powerful as the federal government. But the odds got much better when, in 1916, the group chose a leader who had an unusual credential for a religious chief: he was a lawyer—and a damn good one.

Joseph Rutherford was born in 1869 and showed an early interest in the law, working his way through college as a court stenographer and later becoming a trial lawyer and prosecutor in his home state of Missouri. He was drawn to the Watch Tower Society doctrines in his early twenties. In 1906 he became a baptized Bible Student and the following year became the legal counsel for the Watch Tower Society.

Rutherford's understanding of the court system, constitutional law, and the rights of the individual under the law was so astute that he was soon nicknamed "Judge" Rutherford by both his supporters and his adversaries. Although Rutherford spent time in prison during the group's run-in with the federal government in the Espionage Act conviction, the masterful way he faced that legal battle and many others over the decades became a model for small groups and individuals seeking to establish their societal rights against heavy odds via the court system. (Besides his legal acumen, Rutherford is credited with devising the system of requiring all Witnesses to distribute literature and preach door to door under a centralized organized system.)

Under Rutherford's leadership the Jehovah's Witnesses did not simply react to perceived government intrusions; the group pursued an aggressive, proactive strategy of seeking out ways to limit government power—because all government, Rutherford believed, was an essentially evil force (ruled directly by Satan) that would be destroyed during Armageddon. Rutherford's attitude about government is said to have hardened as a result of his Espionage Act conviction and imprisonment.

The Witnesses objected not only to military service and reciting the Pledge, but to all government-dictated signs of acquiescence. And it was Rutherford who preached a virulent objection to what he perceived as the "idolatry" practiced by Catholics, themselves a persecuted minority until the great migration of the late nineteenth and early twentieth centuries.

Needless to say, the Witnesses became the focus of considerable hostility within many American communities. And it didn't help the group's reputation that they were committed to promoting their beliefs by going door to door, especially on Sunday, and distributing printed publications such as the group's semimonthly magazine, *Watchtower*. In fact, many local communities tried to abolish the practice by applying antipeddling ordinances to the Jehovah's Witnesses. Members were routinely fined, arrested, and often imprisoned under these laws.

While many Witnesses initially accepted this treatment as a sort of martyrdom for their religious commitment, Rutherford and others became increasingly militant. They considered their treatment unfair and illegal, and by the 1930s began a coordinated offensive against the various attacks on the sect's members. Unpopular, small in size, and lacking any type of political influence, the Jehovah's, through Rutherford, came to believe that their best ally was part of the evil government itself: the judicial system.

The legal arguments the Witnesses emphasized in all their cases centered on constitutional protections of freedom of the press (for the cases involving distribution of their printed materials), freedom of speech, and freedom of religion.

In 1935 the Jehovah's Witnesses embarked on a focused campaign against the Pledge. This concentrated effort was sparked by two events.

First, Nazi Germany began its persecution of Witnesses when they refused to perform the "Heil Hitler" salute. (This persecution ultimately resulted in some ten thousand Witnesses being sent off to concentration camps.) The Witnesses saw similarities between that enforced action of the Nazis and the mandatory American flag Pledge of the outstretched hand. It made little difference that the American arm salute had the palm facing upward and the Nazi salute had the palm facing downward; the similarities were far too striking to be ignored.

Second, Carleton Nicholls, Jr., a Witness student in Lynn, Massachusetts, was expelled from his public school in September 1935. Not only was the eight-year-old boy expelled for not saying the Pledge, but his father and a friend of his father's (a non-Witness who was a nephew of the philosopher William James) showed up one day in the classroom with the boy and all three of them refused to participate in the Pledge ceremony. The police were called. The two adults were roughed up, arrested, and trotted off to jail.

Witness leader Rutherford used a scheduled October 6, 1935, radio speech to express his outrage about the Nicholls case. He linked it to the growing persecution of Witnesses in Nazi Germany and warned that a flag salute of any type, to any nation, was an act of true evil. Rutherford told his followers that the nations of the world "are under control of Satan the Devil" and that the flag salute delivered a Witness into the arms of the devil:

> The law of the nation or government that compels the child of God to salute the national flag compels that person to salute the Devil as the invisible god of the nation.

The Rutherford speech was a "call to arms" for Witnesses to begin an aggressive stand against participating in the Pledge ceremony. But given the oath's widespread popularity and the already contentious reputation of the Witnesses, it's not surprising that Rutherford's words were greeted with ferocious antipathy by both the general public and the judges who were called upon to rule in cases that the Witnesses were able to get into court.

In the Carleton Nicholls case against the school district of Lynn, the Massachusetts Supreme Court ruled unanimously in favor of the school board and confirmed the right of the school to expel students who refused to participate in the Pledge salute. Moreover, the court, in its written decision, adamantly found no violation of religious freedom in a mandatory obligation for reciting the Pledge:

> The flag salute and Pledge of allegiance here in question do not in any just sense relate to religion. . . . They do not concern the view of any one as to his Creator. They do not touch upon his relations with his Maker. They impose no obligations as to religious worship. . . . There is nothing in the salute or the Pledge of allegiance which constitutes an act of idolatry, or which approaches to any religious observance. It does not in any reasonable sense hurt, molest, or restrain a human being in respect to "worshipping God" within the meaning of the words in the Constitution.

Of the dozen major cases that the Witnesses were involved in against school districts, most of the court decisions echoed the Nicholls opinion by the Massachusetts high court: there was nothing at all religious about the Pledge or the requirement that it be recited; it was, instead, a rightful patriotic act. In this case and in most of the Witnesses' other court battles the group was supported by the ACLU, which had its roots as an advocacy group defending conscientious objectors to military service during World War I. Formed in 1920 with a stated mission "to defend and preserve the individual rights and liberties guaranteed to every person in this country by the Constitution and laws of the United States," the ACLU has pursued this goal through the court system with a diligence that has frustrated many a "patriot."

The early cases that the Witnesses and the ACLU pursued yielded very little court agreement with their perspective. In fact, a few courts added the opinion that people who were willing to partake in free public education should be required to follow the rules of the public school system. For example, a decision of the New Jersey Supreme Court in a Jehovah's Witnesses case put it bluntly: "Those who do not desire to conform with the demands of the statute can seek their schooling elsewhere."

This is indeed what happened. As more and more Jehovah's Witnesses children were expelled from the public school system, the Witnesses started setting up "Kingdom Schools" in several states that had been chosen by Rutherford's legal team as possible places that would get them the prize they were looking for. Namely, the chance to take their argument to the U.S. Supreme Court. They could then focus on Witness children in the public school without worrying that they would miss an education while their elders fought over them in court.

Finally, while the number of Kingdom Schools grew to accommodate the larger numbers of Witness children expelled from public schools across the nation, the Witnesses and their partner the ACLU found the case they were looking for in Minersville, Pennsylvania, a small town located halfway between Harrisburg and Allentown in the heart of Pennsylvania's hardscrabble coal mining country.

The case started when, following the appeal of Rutherford's October 1935 radio address to abstain from the Pledge ceremony, Witness member Walter Gobitas told his children, William and Lillian, not to say the Pledge at school. (Though the family's last name was Gobitas—spelled with an *a* not an *i*—because of a typo in the papers of the initial court filing, the misspelling is forever frozen in legal history; for consistency we will use "Gobitis" when referring to the family and the case throughout the remainder of this book.)

Ultimately, the Gobitis case would reach the Supreme Court in the Pledge's first national test of its constitutionality.

As soon as the Gobitis children were expelled from the Minersville school—on November 6, 1935, when the family presented its Pledge objections to the local school board, which rejected their arguments, which prompted the superintendent to stand up and expel them on the spot—the legal team at Witnesses headquarters in Brooklyn jumped at the opportunity to see this case through the court system.

They knew the legal situation in Pennsylvania was different from other jurisdictions.

For one thing, the Keystone State did not have a statute compelling Pledge compliance for its public school students. The Minersville school district followed the ceremony out of custom, which included, coincidentally, the school district superintendent's adamant requirement of adherence to that custom. Thus, expelling the Gobitis children was more "arbitrary and capricious" than in states with specific laws.

Also, the Witnesses gambled that there was a larger than normal support of their position among the general public in southeastern Pennsylvania, which had an unusually high percentage of antimilitarian Quakers than nearly any other place in the nation. And, in fact, this assumption was true. There was a small, but growing, tolerance of the Witnesses' perspective. So when Lillian Gobitis stood up in class and declared that she would not recite the Pledge, her teacher embraced the child and commended her on her valor. Then, as school officials dug their heels in deeper in their insistence on their position, local newspaper editorials started expressing support of *voluntary* acceptance of the Pledge ceremony.

The Witnesses' gamble paid off when the federal judge randomly assigned to the case turned out to be a Quaker. It was clear from the beginning of the arguments in the case that Judge Albert Branson Maris had absolutely no sympathy for the Minersville school district's position.

And in his 1938 decision, nearly three years after the matter started, Judge Maris did not mince words about a mandatory Pledge of Allegiance:

> . . . the flag salute by children who are sincerely opposed to it upon conscientious religious grounds is not a reasonable method of teaching civics . . . but tends to have the contrary effect upon such children. . . . Our country's safety surely does not depend upon the totalitarian idea of forcing all citizens into one common mold of thinking and acting or requiring them to render a lip service of loyalty in a manner which conflicts with their sincere religious convictions.

This was a major victory for the Witnesses and the ACLU and it introduced into the debate what had not been allowed by all the other previous judicial determinations: that forced patriotism could violate a religious belief. Up to now the courts deemed the Pledge debate a secular one because nothing in the Pledge, or in its forced recitation, mentioned God or religion. Judge Maris had ruled that it was enough that certain people, in this case the Witnesses, believed that a political practice could violate a religious belief.

The Minersville school board reacted by immediately filing an appeal on the decision. In late 1939, four years after the initial incident, the appeals court upheld the Maris decision and confirmed the ruling against the Minersville school district.

Because the Witnesses won on this appeal, it meant that they would not be able to take this particular case on to the U.S. Supreme Court as the test case they had been hoping to find.

But in an odd chain of events, the Minersville school board, angered to fury and now financially backed by the American Legion as well as a now-defunct group called the Association of Patriotic Societies of Schuykill County, voted to apply to the U.S. Supreme Court to reconsider the case. And in early 1940 the Court agreed to hear it.

9. A VICTORY FOR JEHOVAH

The first oral arguments about the Pledge were presented to the U.S. Supreme Court on April 25, 1940. While the number of incidents of protest over the Pledge had grown over the previous several years and spread to many communities, the controversies were viewed as isolated local problems. Local, that is, until *Minersville School District v. Gobitis* reached the Supreme Court.

Now the American public had started to pay attention to the issues underlying the opposing views. In part, the American psyche was turning away from the consuming financial concerns of the Great Depression and was increasingly focused on troubling world events and the related role of nationalism—both within the United States and abroad. Newspapers followed the case with blow-by-blow descriptions. Editorials in newspapers, general magazines, as well as scholarly and special-interest publications started expressing opinions and strong support of one side of the issue or the other.

"Judge" Rutherford presented part of the oral arguments himself in front of the Supreme Court in defense of the Witnesses' position. The Witnesses had picked up outside support beyond the help of the ACLU when the Bill of Rights Committee of the American Bar Association filed an amici curiae (friend of the court) brief in support of the Witnesses. "[T]he compulsion of a child to participate in a ceremony which he considers idolatrous worship cannot be brushed aside as raising no issue of religious liberty," it said. As David Manwaring pointed out in his classic 1962 work, *Render Unto Caesar: The Flag-Salute Controversy,* the brief, thought to be written by Harvard professor Zechariah Chafee, Jr., was "a direct assault on the bases of [Justice Felix] Frankfurter's *Gobitis* opinion. . . . Chafee also slapped at Frankfurter's reliance on the political processes to correct abuses, noting the political helplessness of Jehovah's Witnesses." Wrote Chafee: "Such a small religious group is very unlikely to attain sufficient voting power to overthrow compulsory flag salute laws. It must obtain protection from the Bill of Rights, or nowhere."

The Witnesses arguments repeated the basic positions that had been successful in the lower courts in Pennsylvania; namely, that they were allowed by the First Amendment to practice their religion. And they were protected under the Fourteenth Amendment from being singled out as a group by state or local laws for special adverse treatment. The Fourteenth Amendment, passed after the Civil War to protect the rights of newly freed slaves from discriminatory state and local laws, had become a powerful tool to protect minority groups by extending national rights to all localities. In many ways, the amendment was the straw that broke the back of the states' rights camel and would become an especially powerful weapon in the civil rights dramas of the 1960s.

The Minersville school board lawyers argued that the Pledge did not violate religious freedom because it made no reference to a religious matter. "The act of saluting the national flag at daily school exercises can not be made a religious rite by the respondents' mistaken interpretation of the Bible," argued Minersville. There was nothing wrong in teaching children, even requiring them to learn, a little national loyalty. It was not just good for the country, it was a necessity:

> Any breakdown in the *esprit de corps* or morale of this country may conceivably have a more devastating

effect upon the nation than a catastrophe resulting from disease, breach of peace, or even an invasion of the realm.

The briefs were presented and the oral arguments made in late April 1940. And over the next month, the justices wrangled.

Often during Supreme Court deliberations a single individual justice will emerge as a highly influential, dominant figure on a case, setting the decision-making path in a particular direction. In the *Gobitis* case, Justice Frankfurter served in that role. And it was an unexpected one.

Frankfurter, a nonpracticing Jew whose father was a rabbi, moved with his family to the United States from his native Austria in 1894 at the age of twelve. His family settled in the predominately Jewish neighborhood of New York City's Lower East Side. Knowing no English, Frankfurter struggled along with other immigrants to assimilate into American life and, in Horatio Alger style, broke anti-Semitic barriers, excelled at P.S. 25 on the Lower East Side, and went on to graduate from the City College of New York before going to Harvard. He graduated with a law degree from Harvard Law School in 1906 and would later became a professor at Harvard, specializing in administrative law, but not before throwing himself into politics. Frankfurter campaigned for Theodore Roosevelt's Bull Moose Progressive Party in 1912 and was one of the founders of the American Civil Liberties Union, which, of course, would become a principal legal ally of the Jehovah's Witnesses in their anti-Pledge campaign.

With his academic credentials and liberal political perspective, Frankfurter found a place in President Franklin Roosevelt's New Deal government, serving as an informal, yet influential White House adviser at the beginning of the New Deal. In 1938, Roosevelt appointed Frankfurter to the U.S. Supreme Court.

Frankfurter's appointment to the Court came on the heels of Roosevelt's unsuccessful attempt the year before to expand the number of Supreme Court justices in order to tip the balance of ideology on the court so that its rulings would be more sympathetic to Roosevelt's New Deal agenda, some of which the Court had rejected. Roosevelt wanted an immediate and expanded opportunity to appoint his own judicial allies and counter the influence that he derisively called the "nine old men." Ironically, federal judges, including Supreme Court justices, were holding on to their positions longer than usual because in the early 1930s Roosevelt had been successful in cutting the pensions of retired judges in half.

Roosevelt claimed that presidents had the power to appoint additional Supreme Court justices for every sitting member over the age of seventy and a half, up to a maximum of an additional six judges. The proposal, famously dubbed the "court-packing plan," was soundly defeated—the Senate voted 70 to 20 to send the bill back to the Judiciary Committee, from which it did not reemerge.

Beginning in late 1938, however, the natural forces of death and voluntary retirement ultimately gave Roosevelt the opportunity to shift the political perspective on the country's highest court. While it is generally agreed that Roosevelt didn't achieve his full goal of majority control of the Supreme Court until 1941, his appointment of Felix Frankfurter was considered at the time to have been an important step in the process.

Frankfurter had been on the high court's bench for less than two years when the *Gobitis* case arrived, and it was expected that his perspective would favor his ACLU roots and the Witnesses. But when the decision was announced, on June 3, 1940, it was clear that Frankfurter, who authored the decision, had switched hats. He had suddenly become a supporter of "judicial restraint," which was the tendency to uphold a law whenever possible, even when a constitutional right might have been violated, in order to support local legislative prerogative. In fact, though the term had been around since the nineteenth century, Frankfurter would become known as a "model of judicial restraint" because of his stand in the *Gobitis* case. He favored filtering national rights through the laws enacted by local elected officials, the Fourteenth Amendment notwithstanding. Judicial restraint, Frankfurter and others believed, was the best way of ascertaining the correctness of the collective wisdom, the will of the people. The intricacies of his judicial restraint philosophy were often lost on the general public, but in this case, it meant that the Minersville School District won. While the exercise of judicial restraint in the *Gobitis* case would later spark further controversial actions, most notably in the high court's 2000 decision to intervene in Florida to guarantee that George W. Bush would win the presidency, *Gobitis* set the standard by which future cases would be judged.

In the 8 to 1 *Gobitis* decision, Frankfurter showed the concept of judicial restraint in action by expressing a firm reluctance to interfere with existing local laws. "The courtroom is not the arena for debating issues of educational policy," he wrote. The language of the decision implied, and was certainly interpreted by many people at the time, that the need to establish national unity among citizens was more important than the possible, but unreasonable, positions of individual liberties. "National unity is the basis of national security," he wrote. "To deny the legislature the right to select appropriate means for its attainment presents a totally different order of position from that of the property of subordinating the possible ugliness of littered streets to the free expression of opinion through handbills."

Frankfurter also rejected the claim that mandatory compliance with saluting the flag compromised religious beliefs:

> Conscientious scruples have not, in the course of
> the long struggle for religious freedom toleration,

relieved the individual from obedience to a general law.

Then Frankfurter expressed a specific opinion about the flag and its importance as a symbol:

> The flag is the symbol of our national unity, transcending all internal differences.

The sole dissenter in the Minersville decision was Justice Harlan F. Stone, a Calvin Coolidge appointee who had served on the Court since 1925. Perhaps one of the most conservative members of the court at the time, Stone emphatically rejected the notion that "national unity" trumped individual freedom:

> The guarantees of civil liberty are but guarantees of freedom of the human mind and spirit and of reasonable freedom and opportunity to express them. . . . The very essence of the liberty which they guarantee is the freedom of the individual from compulsion as to what he shall think and what he shall say. . . .

Stone's lone voice of dissent was drowned out by a wave of fury and violent actions against the Jehovah's Witnesses.

Thousands of Witness children were expelled from schools across the nation. In some communities, Witnesses were rounded up and jailed for sedition or run out of town. A sheriff in one Southern town who had helped escort some sixty Witnesses to the city limits famously remarked to a reporter, "They're traitors. The Supreme Court says so. Ain't you heard?"

The ACLU recorded violent actions against Witnesses in some three hundred communities across the nation, ranging from an incident of tarring and feathering a Witness in Wyoming to castration of a Witness in Nebraska to public beatings overseen by police and city officials in Texas and Illinois.

One of the largest displays of violence occurred just a few days after the Supreme Court decision, when a mob of some twenty-five hundred people in Kennebunk, Maine, rampaged through the town, attacking Witnesses' homes and ultimately sacking and burning down the town's Kingdom Hall, the name of the groups' place of worship. A similar mob of some one thousand people stormed the Kingdom Hall in Klamath, Oregon.

Eleanor Roosevelt made a public plea for calm and called for a halt to the violence against the Witnesses.

Newspapers and magazines debated the issue at length on their editorial pages. Increasingly, as the violence got uglier, the mood changed to expressions of doubt about the Supreme Court's decision. This was particularly true among religious publications. For example, the *Christian Science Monitor* said:

> A voluntary unity of 99 per cent makes the flag a more impressive symbol than an artificial "unity" of 100 per cent.

Felix Frankfurter's friends at the ACLU and *The New Republic,* a liberal periodical that he had written for prior to joining the high court, were particularly critical of the decision, thus isolating Frankfurter from the liberal mainstream that dominated Washington during the Roosevelt years. And within a few months of the barrage of violence against the Witnesses and editorial condemnation of the decision, three of the justices who had voted with Frankfurter recanted their decisions. The three newly dissenting justices were Hugo Black, William Douglas, and Frank Murphy. Perhaps influenced by the torrent of violence, the three justices made an unprecedented joint announcement that their vote in the case was wrong. The public recanting was expressed as part of a June 1942 dissenting opinion involving a case about Witnesses being charged special licensing fees in three states—Alabama, Arkansas, and Arizona—for distributing their religious materials. Although the case was decided against the Witnesses, Justices Black, Douglas, and Murphy now stated that this related case made it clear to them that they had been wrong in *Gobitis*:

> The opinion of the Court sanctions a device which in our opinion suppresses or tends to suppress the free exercise of a religion practiced by a minority group. . . . *Minersville School Dist. v. Gobitis* . . . against the same religious minority is a logical extension of the principles upon which that decision is related. Since we joined in the opinion in the *Gobitis* Case, we think this is an appropriate occasion to state that we now believe that it was also wrongly decided.

This change of position infuriated Frankfurter. He started calling the three judges who changed their minds "the Axis," a particularly nasty comment given the horrors of Hitler and his allies—the Axis—at the time. But Frankfurter maintained his view that the Pledge expressed the importance of loyalty to the United States and that was of utmost importance during World War II. Others, however, lauded the decision of the three judges to change their minds—who were helped by the agreement of new Justice Robert Jackson (who had replaced Charles Evans Hughes in July of 1941)—as well as Stone.

The Witnesses were encouraged in their struggle by the growing number of editorial comments denouncing the *Gobitis* decision, particularly in influential scholarly publications. The *Harvard Educational Review* said that the decision "goes quite as far toward the subordination of the civil liberties of minorities to the will of the majority as any other decision of the Supreme Court."

And in what must have been a surprising amount of support from a longtime religious adversary, the law journals of Catholic schools took a hard stand against the *Gobitis* decision. *Fordham Law Review, Georgetown Law Journal, Jurist, Notre Dame Lawyer,* St. Johns *Law Review,* and University of Detroit *Law Journal* each published scathing denunciations of the *Gobitis* decision. In the Catholic publication *America* this perspective was summarized:

> Lillian and Walter Gobitis are inconsiderable persons. But their case is the case of every man who holds that freedom in education and religion are our most precious rights.

All the opposition meant that a *new* case, raising similar issues, would have to work its way through the procedural process of the court system from an initial suit—perhaps on a local level with someone's arrest by a municipality—through trials at lower court levels, then on to an appeal and then, if one party in the suit or another had the appetite to continue the battle without coming to some arbitrated agreement, ultimately on to the U.S. Supreme Court.

There were no lack of opportunities for the Witnesses to find adversaries to challenge in court. Immediately after the *Gobitis* decision was declared, many states and local communities passed new laws requiring Pledge conformity or tightened existing laws with stronger language. Also, the incidents of punishment for not performing the Pledge as required became more stringent and more widely enforced. The lower courts became more certain about ruling against any type of challenge to the Pledge (in any form) and widely cited the *Gobitis* decision.

The Witnesses, however, kept up their legal battles and were particularly heartened by the public support of the justices who had previously voted against their arguments.

The perfect situation surfaced in West Virginia in January

1942, when the State Board of Education passed a statewide requirement for participation in the Pledge ceremony. The wording of the requirement was directed specifically at the Jehovah's Witnesses and included language that was a direct paraphrasing of the Frankfurter decision in the *Gobitis* case. The state board's resolution stated, for example, that "national unity is the basis of national security" and "conscientious scruples have not in the course of the long struggle for religious toleration relieved the individual from obedience to the general law. . . ."

The law struck a particular chord of dissent in West Virginia because there was an unusually large number of Jehovah's Witnesses living in the state. The original founder of the sect that became the Jehovah's Witnesses, Charles Taze Russell, had lived in Pittsburgh and the first following that he attracted spread geographically into southwestern Pennsylvania and West Virginia.

The law passed in West Virginia said, in part, that "conscientious scruples have not in the course of the long struggle for religious toleration relieved the individual from obedience to the general law not aimed at the promotion or restriction of religious beliefs. . . ." It went on to emphasize the importance of promoting "national unity" as part of the goal of teaching citizenship among schoolchildren and, specifically, that "refusal to salute the Flag be regarded as an act of insubordination, and shall be dealt with accordingly."

Once the West Virginia resolution was passed, local public school districts started expelling Witnesses' children who continued to refuse to salute the flag. Among those expelled were seven children from three Witness families in Charleston. The Barnette family had few financial resources due to Walter Barnette's uneven employment as a pipe fitter. But with the support of the Witnesses's lawyers and the ACLU, it would be the Barnette name that ultimately became associated with the next Pledge case to reach the Supreme Court. The original suit filed in the district court in West Virginia was actually a class action suit filed on behalf of all the students expelled within the state. Later it would become focused primarily on the Barnette situation.

It took from early 1942, when the Barnette children were expelled, until early 1943, for the case to reach the U.S. Supreme Court.

The state lost in the lower courts. The decision of the lower court to uphold the right of the Witnesses' children to refuse to recite the pledge followed the interpretation of the Fourteenth Amendment that the Witnesses's lawyers and the ACLU lawyers had hoped for. The district court decision said in part: "The salute to the flag is an expression of the homage of the soul. To force it upon one who has conscientious scruples against giving it, is petty tyranny unworthy of the spirit of this Republic and forbidden, we think, by the fundamental law."

Having lost the case on this judicial level, it was the State of West Virginia that applied to the Supreme Court for their case to be heard. Thus, the case is known as *West Virginia State Board of Education v. Barnette.*

By the time oral arguments started, on March 11, 1943, most court observers and scholars believed that the Court would overturn *Gobitis.* Since four justices had already proclaimed publicly that they believed the *Gobitis* decision was wrong, only one other justice was needed to render a decision to overrule. Justice Harlan Stone had already expressed his opinion about the issue in his original dissenting opinion in *Gobitis* and Justices Black, Douglas, and Murphy had publicly stated that they had voted incorrectly in the *Gobitis* case. The only question was would there be another vote to overturn the earlier decision.

It's important to consider that the makeup of the Supreme Court had changed dramatically in the few years between the *Gobitis* case and the *Barnette* case. There were two new justices on the court—Robert Jackson, who had been the U.S. attorney general, and Wiley Blount Rutledge, a Kentucky minister and lawyer whom Roosevelt had appointed to the U.S. District Court of Appeals in Washington. And Harlan Stone, the sole dissenter in *Gobitis,* had been elevated to chief justice after the retirement of Charles Hughes in 1941.

The arguments made in the *Barnette* case varied little from the arguments presented in the *Gobitis* case—religious freedom, freedom of speech, due process. The lawyers representing the West Virginia side quoted the Frankfurter decision in *Gobitis* at length and argued that the *Barnette* case was essentially the same.

The Witnesses had lost its longtime leader and legal kingpin, "Judge" Rutherford, before this rehearing of their argument. He had died on January 8, 1942. For the *Barnette* case, the Witnesses repeated the arguments concerning religious freedom and constitutional rights under the Fourteenth Amendment. Then the Witnesses added arguments that directly addressed the issue of "judicial restraint." Calling reliance on popular opinion through legislative process to change "foolish legislation" a failure to protect the constitutional liberties of minority groups, the Witnesses argued that it was the constitutional duty of the Supreme Court to correct laws that created inequities. At one point the Witnesses' lawyer compared Frankfurter's policy of judicial restraint to the actions of Pontius Pilate when he washed his hands of making a decision against the crowd's call for the execution of Jesus.

Frankfurter was furious about the clear direction the case seemed to be taking. He railed against the Court's Axis and repeated his arguments in ever more forceful terms. But this time his arguments fell on deaf ears. In fact, an antagonistic feeling among a few of the justices against Frankfurter lingered from that moment until he retired from the Court in 1962.

The decision was announced, symbolically, on Flag Day, June 14, 1943. The ruling to overturn the *Gobitis* decision was 6–3. Frankfurter wrote a scathing dissent, repeating his judicial restraint perspective by arguing the overriding importance of legislative laws passed by elected representatives. The high court's job, he believed, was to interpret the Constitution, not to overturn local laws. The other two dissenters who voted with Frankfurter did not make public statements.

The majority opinion reflected the wartime mood. It obliquely compared the freedoms of American democracy against the rising evidence of the totalitarian behavior of Nazi Germany. The Court also tried to distance itself from a Nazi German court that had declared Witnesses who refused to perform the "Heil Hitler" salute in violation of the law. At the time, most Americans were self-consciously trying to distinguish their patriotic traditions from those of Germany. Just the year before the outstretched arm salute had been eliminated to avoid any resemblance to the Nazi salute. The hand-over-the-heart gesture that replaced it was encouraged by President Roosevelt, who reminded the people that Abraham Lincoln put his hand to his heart to show honor to the flag during the dedication ceremonies at Gettysburg in 1863.

The majority decision was written by newcomer Robert Jackson, fresh from his one-year stint as attorney general. In fact, Jackson's predecessor as attorney general was Frank Murphy, who had been appointed to the Court just the year before (February 5, 1940) and was among "the Axis" that overturned *Gobitis*. Jackson was no sympathizer. In a commencement address at his alma mater, Albany Law School, in June of 1941, he clearly rejected the notion that the Constitution was some kind of straitjacket:

> Of course our constitutional system is no ready-made garment for peoples of different stature and station. There is a culture and habit of the constitution among our people quite as vital to stability and freedom as the written law of the Constitution. We

lawyers must maintain not alone the integrity of the system but the integrity of the public opinion and understanding which supports the constitutional system.

But he also signaled a clear determination to honor and respect core American values. And he used the war then raging in Europe to make the point. "The values that the Nazi prizes are not our values," he told the graduates. "We prize too much for them the lives of our young men. We do shrink from war. Hitler does not. We do have confidence in legal processes. Hitler does not." After World War II, Jackson would serve as chief U.S. prosecutor in the Nuremburg trials of Nazi leaders.

Without specifically mentioning Nazi Germany in the *Barnette* case majority decision, Jackson said:

> Those who begin coercive elimination of dissent soon find themselves exterminating dissenters. Compulsory unification of opinion achieves only the unanimity of the graveyard. It seems trite but necessary to say that the First Amendment to our Constitution was designed to avoid these ends by avoiding these beginnings. . . . To believe that patriotism will not flourish if patriotic ceremonies are voluntary and spontaneous instead of a compulsory routine is to make an unflattering estimate of the appeal of our institutions.

The decision did not prompt the type of violence that the *Gobitis* decision had. The question of mandatory recitation of the Pledge had finally been resolved, having been brought to lower courts in some twenty states over the decade before the *Barnette* decision. In the 1930s and 1940s the Witnesses alone brought almost forty cases to the Supreme Court. Following the *Barnette* ruling, numerous cases against the Witnesses in the pipeline were dropped or reversed.

But the *Barnette* decision did not stop continued efforts to make the Pledge a required part of American life.

The controversies and strong feelings expressed on both sides of the issue revealed the powerful attachment that the large majority of Americans had to the Pledge and the patriotic feelings it expressed. For politicians viewing this broad-based display of allegiance not only to the flag but to the Pledge itself, it offered an issue that could be translated into something more tangible than philosophical musings of Supreme Court decisions; namely, votes.

10. POLITICAL BATTLES

The political game of patriotic one-upmanship through the use of patriotic symbols has been part of the American landscape at least since Betsy Ross came up with a flag design that George Washington felt expressed the fledgling country's principals better than any of the competing flags being promoted by his political rivals.

And so it is with the Pledge of Allegiance. In fact, the birth of the Pledge and its first use as a special feature of a celebratory event has definite overtones of political maneuvering and grandstanding. As we know, Francis Bellamy convinced President Benjamin Harrison to authorize the Pledge after first getting Harrison's past (and future) opponent Grover Cleveland to throw his weight behind it. And Harrison wisely used his position as sitting president to win that round of the match— although he lost his next presidential bid to Cleveland. The real winner, of course, was Bellamy, since this act by Harrison was the beginning of the legend that cemented Bellamy's Pledge in the American consciousness.

While politicians have used the Pledge for decades as a political football, various groups and individuals (both within the political spectrum and outside) have tried to add, subtract, reposition, reinterpret, contest, and embrace the oath, from a multiplicity of viewpoints, to express their particular political perspectives or gain political advantages. An antiabortion group, for instance, would like the Pledge to be rewritten to say "with liberty and justice for all, born and unborn." Some women's rights advocates would like to see the wording altered to say, "with liberty and justice for all men and women." Another group gathered considerable support in the early 1970s to add the word "responsibilities" to the Pledge so that it would end with a reminder of duty toward a national commitment: "with liberty, justice and *responsibilities* for all."

As these different points of view jockey for a position around the oath to the flag, the courts have been called on to toss around a political hot potato, trying to maintain the appearance of nonpartisanship. But even while nodding toward a court's objectivity, we recognize the essential political strings attached to the courts each time a president appoints a new Supreme Court justice and we are treated to the spectacle—more so in recent years—of partisan questioning by members of the Senate Judiciary Committee. Though there have been many "surprises" with such appointments, it is no secret that presidents hope their nominees to the high court will carry on their legacy, and their point of view, long after they have left the White House.

The power of a Supreme Court decision, as well as lower court rulings, is limited, of course, since those decisions do not automatically require a purging and updating of laws. Instead, a Supreme Court decision applies only to the specific situation brought before the Court; its application to other laws or situations is handled on a case-by-case basis, in further court action. Indeed, we are a "nation of laws," but they are laws constantly being challenged, reinterpreted, rewritten, and ignored, as new situations arise, new contexts within which to view those specifics. Though judicial experts often talk about an issue being "settled," in fact, very few are. As we saw in the reversal of the *Gobitis* and *Barnette* cases, the Supreme Court can change its mind.

Actually, in the wake of the *Barnette* decision, some defiant school districts tried to continue enforcing mandatory Pledge participation, citing the minority decision in the Supreme Court case and hoping that the courts would change their minds again.

These defiant actions didn't get very far. The U.S. Justice Department notified all U.S. attorneys in November 1943 that these actions against religious freedom should be dealt with firmly before they ended up in lawsuits.

Still, thousands of laws, including laws mandating Pledge ceremonies, remain "on the books" despite having been deemed unconstitutional by a Supreme Court decision. They remain on the books simply because no one has bothered to challenge them, or, perhaps more commonly, no state or local agency has bothered to enforce the laws and thereby have avoided a legal challenge.

By the late 1940s, however, as America emerged from a patriotic and popular war, there were fewer challenges to mandatory Pledge participation and, once again, the oath enjoyed overwhelming popularity as a central expression of Americanism on the global stage. And politicians soon found the Pledge a perfect instrument for building the nationalism needed to fight the new war, a Cold War that began in the early 1950s and would dominate the world's geopolitics for the next half century. In large part due to the brevity and expressiveness its author bestowed on it, the Pledge became the symbol of perceived basic differences between American ideals and the growing strength and influence of communism in the Soviet Bloc.

But as it was the touchstone of American ideals in the face of godless communism, some found Bellamy's Pledge lacking— lacking, in fact, just two words.

The two words were, of course, "under God."

That the Pledge lacked something was a sentiment that started gathering support after the first recorded use of the added words "under God" during a Pledge recitation on February 12, 1948, at a Lincoln's Birthday celebration in Chicago at the Illinois Society of the SAR. The idea of adding the words is credited to Louis A. Bowman, the chaplain of the Illinois Society. The relevance of introducing the additional words at the Lincoln celebration is that Bowman wanted the Pledge to reflect the words Lincoln had used in his 1863 Gettysburg address:

> this nation, under God, shall have a new birth of freedom and that government of the people, by the people, for the people shall not perish from the earth.

There have been many interpretations of Lincoln's "under God" in this context. One linguistic historian claims that during Lincoln's time people would have understood "under God" to mean "God willing." Whether or not this historic interpretation of linguistics is accurate (and there are scholars who would disagree), by the time Bowman took the initiative to add the deity to the national oath, there seemed little doubt that he meant "God's guidance" or "God's approval" or even "God's acknowledgment of rightness" of the specific nation, the United States. And in the subsequent lobbying effort, those definitions were surely the ones promoted by "under God" proponents to emphasize the difference between the United States and the "godlessness" of the Communist Soviet Union and its satellite countries.

By 1951 the "under God" movement gained great traction when it became a cause of the Knights of Columbus, which gave it the same strong support that the group gave the original Columbus Day celebration. Only now the Knights were a much more powerful organization, representing millions of Catholics and armed with a healthy war chest. Though some of the anti-Catholic sentiment that had been the original motivation behind the formation of the Knights had dissipated by the 1950s, there remained considerable concern about "the Papists" taking over the White House, which is what worried many people when John F. Kennedy ran for president in 1960. It was no small irony that the Pledge, which was born at a time when Catholics were excluded from many of the benefits it trumpeted, would find among twentieth-century Catholics its staunchest supporters. But it didn't hurt that the Pledge was born in a celebration of the group's namesake, Christopher Columbus, the founder of modern America, a Catholic, and Italian.

Added to those already strong bonds, as we saw in the previous chapter, Catholics had no love lost for the Jehovah's Witnesses, who had been a constant burr in the Papists' side for years prior to the Supreme Court Pledge challenge. Beginning in the early part of the twentieth century, Witness leader "Judge" Rutherford waged a war of words against the "idolatry" of Catholics. In turn, Catholics were among the most outspoken groups in support of the high court's ruling against the Witnesses in the *Gobitis* case. (One Catholic parish had organized a boycott of the Gobitas store in Minersville.)

While there does not seem to be any explicit evidence that the Knights promoted "under God" as a direct reaction to the Witnesses' success at the Supreme Court, they didn't need the sect to whet their "under God" fervor. Catholics were among the most ardent anti-Communists in America.

In fact, in early 1951 the Knights made the addition of "under God" a requirement for meetings of the group's highest member level, Fourth Degree Assemblies. And before the end of 1952, the Supreme Council of the Knights of Columbus passed a resolution to require the change in wording at all of the group's meetings. In addition, the Supreme Council sent off copies of their resolution to all government leaders, including the president, urging congressional action to add "under God" to the Pledge.

Coinciding with the Knights' push to include "under God" was a general movement toward public expression of religious worship involving government approval. For example, in 1952 Congress called for a National Day of Prayer to be held annually. President Dwight Eisenhower introduced the National

Prayer Breakfast and Congress set aside a room in the Capitol for prayer. These and other actions might simply have reflected a growing American move toward embracing religion. But whenever a new religious ceremony was added to some public event, it was draped in anticommunism and what was perceived as the growing threat from the Soviet Union. It was God that distinguished the United States from the USSR. In a 1953 speech, President Eisenhower spoke of the special role of God when he said:

> faith is the living source of our spiritual strength. And this strength is our matchless armor in our worldwide struggle against the forces of Godless tyranny and oppression.

There is no doubt that this, like other statements of the time, combined God and politics.

Quite ironically, Eisenhower had been raised a Jehovah's Witness (when it was still called the Tract Society), the very group, of course, that would later call the Pledge of Allegiance a tool of Satan. During his childhood, Eisenhower's parents—particularly his mother, Ida—were active in the Watchtower group. The Eisenhower home in Abilene, Kansas, was routinely used as a meeting place for weekly Bible studies under the Watchtower aegis. Eisenhower turned away from the teachings of the sect when he entered West Point in 1915. But his mother remained an ardent Jehovah's Witness until her death in 1946. Eisenhower's father reportedly drifted away from the sect, but when he died in 1942, he was given a full Jehovah's Witness funeral. In one of the more bizarre familial contradictions in American presidential history—and there have been many—Eisenhower's mother, who as a Jehovah's Witness was antiwar, expressed during her lifetime a pride in her son's accomplishments but also a disappointment that he had pursued a military career. Despite the scrutiny that political leaders undergo concerning their religious affiliations, Eisenhower's religious background, no doubt because of savior status as an American general in World War II, was never questioned.

When asked about his religious background, Eisenhower provided a vague description of growing up in a household that followed strict biblical scripture. In fact, he professed no official connection to any religious group prior to his election as president. It wasn't until thirteen days after his inauguration that he was baptized, confirmed, and entered into membership of the Presbyterian faith. He then regularly attended church service at the New York Avenue Presbyterian Church in Washington, D.C. This Presbyterian membership would later serve as a critical deciding factor for Eisenhower's support for adding "under God" to the Pledge.

In the spring of 1953 the first congressional resolution was introduced to officially add "under God" to the Pledge. Several other resolutions were introduced over the next year but failed to generate enough enthusiasm or support to get through the committee process even to be voted on.

Then, on February 7, 1954, a single event propelled the movement into a snowball that culminated in the official addition of "under God" to the Pledge on Flag Day, June 14, 1954.

The event was an impassioned sermon commemorating Lincoln's birthday given by the Reverend George MacPherson Docherty at the New York Avenue Presbyterian Church, the very congregation Dwight Eisenhower had joined just two years earlier. Abraham Lincoln himself had frequently attended services in the church, and there was a traditional Lincoln pew that on February 7, 1954, was occupied by Dwight and Mamie Eisenhower.

While the Catholic Knights of Columbus had set the groundwork for adding "under God" to the Pledge, what sealed the deal was a Presbyterian minister who literally had the president's ear.

In an electrifying and rousing sermon, Docherty hit every point of political and religious patriotism of the day. He focused specifically on what he considered the missing element of the Pledge that he noticed when hearing his children recite it:

> There was something missing in this Pledge, and that which was missing was the characteristic and defini- tive factor in the "American Way of Life." Indeed, apart from the mention of the phrase, the United States of America, this could be the Pledge of *any* Republic. In fact, I could hear little Muscovites re- peat a similar Pledge to their hammer and sickle flag in Moscow with equal solemnity, for Russia is also a Republic that claims to have overthrown the tyranny of kingship.

Then Docherty identified the one element that would sepa- rate the Pledge in the United States from one that could be re- cited in Soviet Russia, an element that Abraham Lincoln had insightfully identified nearly one hundred years before:

> It is the one fundamental concept that completely and ultimately separates Communist Russia from the democratic institutions of this Country. This was seen clearly by Lincoln. "One nation UNDER GOD" this people shall know a new birth of freedom. And "UNDER GOD" are the definitive words. . . . We face, today, a theological war. . . . It is . . . a battle of the gods. It is the view of man as it came down to us from the Judeo-Christian civilization in mortal com- bat against modern, secularized, godless humanity. . . . To omit the words "under God" in the Pledge of Allegiance is to omit the definitive character of the "American Way of Life."

Docherty next addressed the issue of the separation of church and state promised in the U.S. Constitution. He interpreted the First Amendment guarantee only as not allowing an official church of the state, not a denial of a supreme being. He wound up his sermon by arguing the continuity of the use of the acknowledgment of God throughout government activities as the logical reason for adding "under God" to the Pledge:

> In Jefferson's phrase, if we deny the existence of the "God who gave us life," how can we live by "the liberty he gave us at the same time"? This is a God fearing nation. On our coins, bearing the imprint of Lincoln and Jefferson, are the words "In God We Trust." Congress is opened with prayer. It is upon the Holy Bible the President takes his oath of office. Naturalized citizens, when they take their oath of allegiance, conclude solemnly, with the words "so help me God."

These same arguments would be used over and over in the future whenever the inclusion of "under God" in the Pledge was contested.

Docherty's sermon was immediately celebrated by Eisenhower and throughout the country. It was reprinted in popular book form. Its influence spread through Congress and, despite some minor squabbling, Congress passed the resolution with almost no opposition.* "I have been most pleased to note in the press a report of the sermon," said Congressman Louis Rabaut (D.-Mich.), who had already introduced the bill "to Amend the Pledge of Allegiance to Include the Phrase 'Under God,'" ad-

---

*An exception was Congressman Kenneth Keating (R.-N.Y.), who objected to the change because it would damage a "work of American literature." But he was representing his constituent David Bellamy, who did not want his father's pledge changed again.

dressing his House colleagues. "You may argue from dawn to dusk about differing political, economic, and social systems, but the fundamental issue which is the unbridgeable gap between America and Communist Russia is a belief in Almighty God." And he summed up perfectly the logic of the anti-Communist fervor of the time:

> From the root of atheism stems the evil weed of communism and its branches of materialism and political dictatorship. Unless we are willing to affirm our belief in the existence of God and His creator-creature relation to man, we drop man himself to the significance of a grain of sand and open the floodgates to tyranny and oppression.

Fittingly, on June 14, 1954, Flag Day—just a few months after Docherty's sermon—Eisenhower signed the bill into law.

Right after the signing, on the steps of the Capitol in Washington, the new Pledge was recited by a group of government officials and representatives from such groups as the American Legion. A bugle rendition of "Onward, Christian Soldiers" followed. The event was carried live on the CBS network with commentator Walter Cronkite declaring it a "stirring event."

The historic influence of Docherty's sermon continued with the related Cold War adoption of the phrase "In God We Trust" as the official motto of the United States, which was signed into law by Eisenhower in 1956.

Both actions were embraced with overwhelming popularity by politician and voters alike, Republicans and Democrats. Embarrassingly for the Democrats, however, a televised recitation of the Pledge during the 1956 Democratic National Convention accidentally left out the phrase "under God." The change in wording took some time to get used to.

While there were a few dissenting voices concerning the

direct official expression of "God" in connection with government, those voices were squelched quickly and effectively. As early as 1957 there was a court case brought by the Freethinkers of America against the New York State commissioner of education asking that the phrase be deleted. The request was summarily denied by using the novel argument, in part, that although the Constitution prohibited a "State Religion," it did not prohibit the development of a "Religious State." And the court suggested that if someone had an objection to the phrase that it was simple enough just not to say it while reciting it.

Although a few other attempts were made to bring the issue to court, it would be fifty years before a concerted effort to challenge the words "under God" would hit the national scene in the Pledge's third trip to the Supreme Court.

But during the years before that case, the Pledge was no less a national political firebrand—beginning in the turbulent 1960s and continuing to this day.

The seemingly cohesive American collective state of mind of the 1950s that gave America an "under God" and an "In God We Trust" slipped away as the Vietnam War heated up and the draft loomed large in the lives of young American men. This controversial military action, combined with the racial unrest and civil rights controversies of the period, as well as rapidly changing social mores that ranged from abortion to widening recreational drug use, began polarizing Americans in a way unseen since, perhaps, the Civil War. This time the polarization was not strictly geographical.

The Pledge once again became a weapon.

On one side, people who opposed the political direction of the country wanted to show their disapproval by abstaining from reciting the Pledge during occasions when the Pledge was traditionally recited. These people even started refusing to stand while the Pledge was being said. In the past, those who refused to say the Pledge generally compromised by standing silently during the recitation.

On the other side, an "America, love it or leave it" mentality boiled up among many people in positions of authority to force the objectors into saying the Pledge or be subject to punishment. The justification for this new round of reprisals was that the Supreme Court decision in the *Barnette* case only permitted Constitutional abstention from reciting the Pledge based on *religious* convictions and not on *political* convictions to serve as a protest. So, for example, in 1963 a group of Black Muslim students in Elizabeth, New Jersey, were suspended for not saying the Pledge because the school board determined that the Black Muslims were not a religious group but were instead a racial and political group and as such were not eligible on religious grounds to refuse to say the Pledge. This case made it to the New Jersey Supreme Court, which ruled that the Black Muslims, whether a religious group or not, could abstain based on any "conscientious scruples."

Teachers who refused to lead their classes in reciting the Pledge or refused to say the Pledge themselves while the class recited it came under particular scrutiny and punishment. Several teachers around the country were dismissed for these actions, but all were ultimately reinstated after courts reviewed the dynamics of the situations. For example in 1970, Susan Russo, a teacher in Henrietta, New York, did not have her contract renewed because she failed to recite the Pledge. (Several students and parents had complained to the school about her behavior.) Russo appealed to the courts to be reinstated. The first court agreed with the school and decided that Russo had failed to perform her required duties as a teacher and had been rightfully dismissed. Russo appealed to a federal court, which decided in her favor, stating that there was no reason students should have more Constitutional rights than teachers. The school board appealed to the Supreme Court for a further decision. But the high court, with its power to pick and choose which cases to hear, refused to take the case, thereby leaving the lower court's decision intact.

Despite these legal setbacks in mandatory participation in reciting the Pledge, the political position of those pursuing the demand that *everyone* say the Pledge remained the dominant popular position.

And in this period when it came to laws dealing with the Pledge, politicians knew and understood this power. Then—and now—once politicians get into positions of legislative power, they can publicly proclaim a popular position on the Pledge and enact laws that reflect that popular position. They can do this with impunity even though they have full knowledge that if the law was ever strictly enforced and then challenged in a court, it would very likely not stand up to legal scrutiny.

That, in a nutshell, is legislative politics.

And as nearly every politician has learned in the last hundred years: woe to those who oppose the popularity of the Pledge of Allegiance—and the laws that promote and protect it.

This unquestionable dictum seemed to evade Michael Dukakis, the Democratic candidate for president in the 1988 election. In 1977, while governor of Massachusetts, Dukakis made a decision about the use of the Pledge in his state that reverberated with such furious intensity during the 1988 campaign that many political observers claim it cost him the election. It all started when the Massachusetts state legislature passed a statute in 1977 replacing a 1935 state law about compulsory recitation of the Pledge in public schools. The new law strengthened and expanded the requirements of the earlier law. The 1935 law required teachers, under penalty of fine and possible dismissal from their jobs, to lead their students in the Pledge at least once a week. The new law made it mandatory for teachers to have their students recite the Pledge daily.

The political popularity of enacting this new law apparently blinded the legislators of 1977 to the events that followed the passage of their own 1935 law.

It was this very 1935 Massachusetts law that prompted the expulsion of Jehovah's Witness Carelton Nicholls, Jr., from his school in Lynn, Massachusetts, which in turn sparked the inflammatory October 1935 radio address by Witness leader (and lawyer) "Judge" Rutherford, which then began the coordinated boycott of the Pledge by Witnesses across the country, leading ultimately to the U.S. Supreme Court decision to declare compulsory Pledge compliance unconstitutional in the 1943 *Barnette* decision.

However, despite all the legal wrestling over the *Nicholls* case in Massachusetts, that particular case never made it to the U.S. Supreme Court to test the 1935 Massachusetts law specifically. (The Witnesses decided not to use the case as the one they focused on.) Since there was no further appeal on the *Nicholls* case, the 1937 ruling of the Massachusetts Supreme Court remained the law in the Bay State, even though it was not, technically, the law of the land. According to the Massachusetts Supreme Court, the Witnesses were wrong about the Pledge:

> There is nothing in the salute or the Pledge of allegiance which constitutes an act of idolatry, or which approaches any religious observance. It does not in any reasonable sense hurt, molest, or restrain a human being in respect to "worshipping God."

Therefore, when the Massachusetts legislature wanted to expand the law in 1977 there had been no further court test on the state's 1935 law since the 1943 Supreme Court decision in the *Barnette* case.

But there was a little wrinkle in the Massachusetts law that would become a political bombshell for future presidential candidate Dukakis. The Massachusetts law made the Pledge compulsory for *teachers*. The *Barnette* decision called the compulsory nature unconstitutional for *students* and said nothing about teachers.

Assuming that a law directed toward teachers was immune to the Supreme Court decision directed to students, the Massachusetts legislature sent the bill on to Dukakis to approve—or to veto. The legislative politicians were then able to go back to their constituents with the proof of their patriotic action by expanding and strengthening the Pledge requirement.

Dukakis, perhaps recognizing that he was now on a political hot seat, turned the matter over to the Massachusetts Supreme Court and the state's attorney general for advisory opinions on the constitutionality of the new law. Both the state's supreme court and the attorney general's office proclaimed it, after reviewing the new law in light of *Barnette,* unconstitutional.

Then, with this apparent bipartisan evidence in hand, Dukakis committed what turned out to be near (if not complete) political suicide: he vetoed the new Pledge law.

The veto was quickly overridden by the Massachusetts legislature and the law remains on the books today as originally written. It has never been tested in court, primarily because it has rarely, if ever, been enforced.

What might have been a minor event in the days of Michael Dukakis's term as governor of Massachusetts turned into one of the most important issues of his 1988 presidential bid.

When George H. W. Bush's Republican strategy team filtered through Dukakis's past for weaknesses to present to the voters, this 1977 Pledge veto surfaced as a political hot button.

Bush used the veto action in his acceptance speech at the Republican convention, saying: "Should public school teachers be required to lead our children in the Pledge of Allegiance? My opponent says no—but I say yes." Then to emphasize the point he finished the speech by leading the crowd in reciting the Pledge.

Dukakis never recovered from this moment. Earlier in the election year, Dukakis led Bush in polls by as much as sixteen percentage points. But as the Republicans hammered the Pledge issue more and more, the issue stuck and delivered perhaps the deciding blow to Dukakis's campaign. In one survey of Democrats in Ohio who originally supported Dukakis and then defected to Bush, 21 percent said they changed their minds because of the Pledge issue that Bush had raised.

To counter this attack, Dukakis tried to provide a defense of his Pledge decision based on constitutional law. Dukakis found, however, that few voters had the patience to follow his scholarly arguments when such arguments couldn't fit on a bumper sticker like "Save the Pledge."

The Bush use of the Pledge as a political weapon was undoubtedly the most dramatic and effective of all time. However, it wasn't the first time it was used in a presidential campaign. In 1964, Republican presidential candidate Barry Goldwater's campaign ran a powerful television commercial that featured images of a classroom of schoolchildren reciting the Pledge intercut with images of Soviet leader Nikita Khrushchev delivering his famous "We will bury you" speech of 1956. In that speech to a group of Western ambassadors visiting Moscow, Khrushchev stormed: "Whether you like it or not, history is on our side. We will bury you." (This oft-quoted line is, however, slightly mistranslated. The actual line was "We will dig you in.") The message of the Goldwater commercial was clear. It would be better to have a nation "under God" than under Khrushchev.

In the Bush/Dukakis struggle, Dukakis actually made things worse for himself when he tried to turn the issue around and portray Bush as a president who would ignore constitutional rights. Answering that charge, Bush simply lashed Dukakis to the American Civil Liberties Union (ACLU), which, as a group, had backed and won Supreme Court cases that have often been largely unpopular among voting Americans—such as, the Pledge case of 1943. In addition, Bush also successfully painted Dukakis as a person who, as president, would likely attempt to appoint people to the Supreme Court predisposed to agreeing with the positions of groups like the ACLU, which, for many people, meant the destruction of beloved American traditions and national beliefs such as the Pledge.

While other factors contributed to Bush's landslide victory over Dukakis, the Pledge issue was certainly one of the nails in Dukakis's political coffin.

Even Congress was forced into the Pledge act that year when, on September 9, Congressman John G. Rowland (R.-Conn.) proposed changing House rules to make the Pledge a regular order of business. His motion was ruled out of order—and the ruling was upheld 226 to 168—but the following Tuesday, feeling the political pinch, in what *The Washington Post* said was "a departure from regular practice," Speaker of the House Jim Wright (D.-Tex.) ordered the Pledge recited.

Said Wright after the vote, sounding defensive, "None of us objects to the Pledge of Allegiance; all of us embrace the Pledge of Allegiance. But I think it is very important that all of us recognize that the Pledge of Allegiance to the flag is something intended to unite us; not intended to divide us. I think all of us and each of us in his heart of hearts would subscribe to the belief that patriotism knows no political party. . . . And surely nothing would be more reprehensible than for any of us to suggest that another member or another citizen simply by reason of adhering to the principles of the other political party, was less patriotic than ourselves.

"Judge Learned Hand said it well," Wright continued. "He said that 'society is already in the process of dissolution where neighbors begin to view one another with suspicion or where nonconformity with accepted creed becomes a mark of disaffection.' Let that not be the epitaph of this civilization."

Such high-minded rhetoric did not prevent Michael Dukakis from fading into the mists of political history. Both George H. W. Bush, the forty-first president, as well as his son George W. Bush, our forty-third president, used the Pledge to great political advantage. But it was an awkward year for the Pledge. Humorist Calvin Trillin weighed in just a month before the 1988 election with a column in the left-leaning *Nation* that began with a girl at the breakfast table demanding, "Daddy, can you recite the Pledge of Allegiance?"

"What kind of cereal do you want this morning? We're pushing this high-fiber stuff—although, as I understand the list of ingredients on the box, I think you could satisfy the same vitamin requirements by chewing on your pencil in math class."

"Come on, Daddy. Just try one time."

"Or you might want some of this kind that's fortified with a couple of years' supply of iron, unless you think it'll weigh you down."

"But aren't people who recite the Pledge of Allegiance more patriotic than other people?"

Trillin makes fun of GOP vice presidential candidate Dan Quayle—infamous for avoiding the Vietnam draft by joining the National Guard and for issuing such malapropisms as "A mind is a terrible thing to lose"—by telling his daughter, "So Dan Quayle is more patriotic than the people who went to Vietnam."

And what about George Washington and Thomas Jefferson and Benjamin Franklin, his daughter asks. She had heard on the "television news" that there was no Pledge until 1892.

"Then they were unpatriotic," said Daddy.

Daddy goes over the history of the Pledge, including the

victorious Jehovah's Witnesses' Supreme Court case. But the daughter persists, asking again why people who recite the Pledge are more patriotic than those who don't.

"As your mother said when I asked her if she knew the name of the Secretary of Labor, I won't stand here and be grilled like a common criminal. . . . I think history might have taken a different turn if Benjamin Franklin had known about riboflavin."

All this popular debate about the use and misuse of the Pledge didn't prevent a new legal challenge to the nation's sacred creed—in fact, it probably contributed to it: a test dipping back to the Eisenhower-era change to the Pledge.

The many direct (and ineffective) objections over the decades to the "under God" addition to the Pledge focused on First Amendment rights separating church and state. Eisenhower's Reverend Docherty made a specific point by insisting that the original idea behind the First Amendment was simply to guard against a government-dictated *official* church—such as the Church of England—and did not mean to remove religion from government sanction. A more commonly accepted interpretation of the First Amendment, however, has been a more strict separation of church and state, and increasingly over the years it has been this argument that has achieved court success; for example, for removing public prayer from schools, forbidding displays of Ten Commandment posters and nativity scenes in public places, and banning prayer in school but allowing observance of moments of silence.

In the early years of challenge to the addition of "under God" to the Pledge, groups such as Buddhists, Unitarian Universalists, secularists, and, of course, atheists found one objection or another to being forced to acknowledge in reciting the Pledge to acknowledge *one* God, a *specific* version of God, or *any* God.

There were also some objections from ardently religious groups. For example, one interfaith group of religious scholars argued that "under God," when uttered in a rote recitation of the Pledge, made God into a generic concept that "lead to a trivialization of faith." Another group argued that if "under God" had become so religiously unimportant when saying the Pledge, then it actually ended up asking students "to take the name of the Lord in vain," which violated one of the Ten Commandments.

Very few people in the vast majority of Americans who support the Pledge in every aspect of its current form have spent much time thinking about the multiplicity of layers of interpretation from one end of the faith spectrum to the other. And that's the political challenge that the courts have tried to dodge since people have attempted to get "under God" judicially defined since the phrase was adopted in 1954.

Several cases worked their way through the court system only to be turned back at the Supreme Court level with the Court's power to pick and choose exactly which cases it will hear.

It wasn't until an unusual situation forced the Supreme Court's hand in 2004 to hear the arguments on both sides.

11. UNDER GOD

The catalyst in the most recent "under God" Supreme Court case was Michael A. Newdow. A practicing physician in San Francisco and a nonpracticing attorney (who would ultimately represent himself before the U.S. Supreme Court), Newdow was (and is) an atheist who confronted the issue of the Pledge because he did not want his young daughter to be forced to acknowledge any God by reciting the Pledge. Also, he argued, it wasn't enough just to have the child refrain from either saying the Pledge in full or saying it at all since he felt that it would cause her to become a focus of scorn by other students and, perhaps, adults. In fact, he stated that simply making his daughter stand and listen to the Pledge violated First Amendment rights.

Similar cases had been brought before various courts in the past arguing similar points; Newdow had the tenacity to keep going. He brought a lawsuit against his daughter's school district of Elk Grove, California. The suit was quickly rebuffed in 2000. But then Newdow presented his position on appeal in 2002 before the U.S. Court of Appeals for the Ninth Circuit.

The Ninth Circuit has jurisdiction over nine states—Alaska, Washington, Idaho, Montana, Oregon, Nevada, California, Hawaii, and Arizona—as well as the Pacific territories of Guam and the Northern Mariana Islands. The large geographic area encompasses a full spectrum of political leanings, from the traditionally liberal areas of San Francisco to the strongly conservative ones of Alaska, making any action about the Pledge ripe for controversy. But no one expected this decision: the Ninth

Circuit actually decided in Newdow's favor. This decision, in post-9/11 America, shocked much of the nation. The court declared that "under God" was unconstitutional and that it violated the Establishment Clause of the First Amendment. The majority decision in this case stated:

> In the context of the Pledge, the statement that the United States is a nation "under God" is an endorsement of religion. It is a profession of a religious belief, namely, a belief in monotheism. . . . The text of the official Pledge, codified in federal law, impermissibly takes a position with respect to the purely religious question of the existence and identity of God. . . .

In addition, the court declared that having schoolchildren recite the Pledge was coercive and that it put children into a position of an "unacceptable choice between participating and protesting."

Few decisions on this appellate level have ever gotten as much immediate political attention as this one did. Congressmen tumbled out of the Capitol in Washington, D.C., literally elbowing each other aside to get to a photogenic position on the Capitol steps to condemn the court's decision and to recite the Pledge for any news camera available.

The Dukakis lesson had been learned. And it was, after all, a congressional election year. Silence on the matter could only be considered anti-Pledge. Movement began almost immediately to introduce a constitutional amendment to protect the Pledge—and its "under God" phrase—from any threat, judicial or legislative.

The case was actually sent back to the Ninth Circuit two more times.

The first rehearing of the case involved the fact that Newdow was not actually married to the child's mother. He also did not have full custody of the child. The mother, Sandra Banning, disagreed with Newdow's position and *wanted* her daughter to believe in God and to recite the Pledge. The mother was previously granted full *legal* custody of the child, meaning the mother had the sole right to make decisions about the child's education and welfare. This first return to the Ninth Circuit was to decide whether or not Newdow even had the right, or the standing, to bring the question of the Pledge to court. The court ruled that Newdow did indeed have the standing to object to unconstitutional government action affecting his child, even though he was a noncustodial parent.

The Elk Grove School District appealed again to the Ninth Circuit asking this time for an *en banc* court hearing—meaning a hearing by all the member judges of the court instead of just a panel of judges as had originally decided on the case. The motion was denied.

With a considerable amount of political support, including a strong statement against the court from President George W. Bush, the Elk Grove School District pushed the case up to the U.S. Supreme Court. The Supreme Court agreed to hear the case. Oral arguments were presented on March 24, 2004.

Unlike the Jehovah's Witnesses, who received financial and legal support from such groups as the ACLU, Newdow weathered his suit almost alone. The ACLU at first didn't think his case was winnable and later decided that the issues were so potentially divisive during a presidential election that raising them would undermine their larger political goals. Newdow solicited help from the American Jewish Congress (AJC), which also refused to help, even though the group had been known to be strong supporters of the separation of church and state. Even the Americans United for Separation of Church and State (AU) refused Newdow's request for support because of a professed lack of resources as well as uneasiness about the political ramifications. Eventually the ACLU and the AU joined in presenting a "friend of the court" brief in support of the Newdow position.

Still, when Newdow entered the courtroom, he was pretty much on his own—and only eight of the nine Supreme Court justices were ready to hear the case. Justice Antonin Scalia recused himself at Newdow's request because Scalia had publicly criticized the Ninth Circuit decision in a speech the year before. There was the possibility, therefore, that the Court could split 4–4 and end up making no decision at all.

Scores of briefs were filed with the Court representing both sides of the issue, including one from the George W. Bush administration throwing full support and legal arguments behind maintaining the "under God" phrase.

As the date neared for oral arguments, I contacted the Court's press office in hopes of getting into the press gallery. The official who turned me down explained that the Court was hard pressed to fill requests even for all the major media representatives because interest in the case was so intense. I decided to go to the capital anyway and hang around the Court to see who I might talk to.

March 23, 2004: the eve of the oral arguments. It was a crisp afternoon in Washington. The Capitol gleamed alabaster white against a limpid blue sky. Across First Street, by the marble steps of the Supreme Court building, I found a group of college students gathered on the sidewalk. They were a smiling bunch, easily approachable. Most were freshmen from George Washington University and American University. They had come to be first in line for the few seats in the Court chamber available to the public.

The students were split down the middle on the "under God" issue. All spoke earnestly and thoughtfully in laying out their positions. A young woman from Long Island saw the phrase as clearly religious with no place in a civic ritual, and a fervent young Unitarian from Connecticut took the same position. A fellow from Puerto Rico said the phrase should be kept in because it reflects the nation's historic beliefs. A government-affairs major from Delaware, who carried a pocket edition of the Constitution, also argued that "under God" should stay in. "It all goes back to John Locke," he said with a gentle smile, "the idea that the rights of mankind come from God."

The calendar said spring, but as the afternoon turned toward dusk a lingering winter chill descended. The rumpled sleeping bags and blankets the students had with them looked as though they would offer flimsy protection for overnight camping on the sidewalk. The young people seemed unconcerned though. They buzzed in anticipation of witnessing the landmark case.

As the evening wore on, someone got on a cell phone to order pizza and succeeded on only the second try to find a place that would deliver to a sidewalk. A tour bus pulled up and members of a church group piled out for a prayer vigil. I left for dinner with friends, and when I came back to check on the students found them as fresh and voluble as ever. One of the churchwomen with a friend living around the corner had invited the students over to warm up and to use the facilities, which they had done in rotation. A long line had formed behind them, with what looked like many more people than would be able to get into the Court the next day. I went back to my friends' place to sleep.

Upon my return, in the half-light of dawn, I found the students looking remarkably chipper, still glowing with excitement. Dominick, the young man with the pocket Constitution and the de facto leader of the group, had a surprise for me. One of the group had left. "You can take his place," Dominick said. Wow. All I had expected was to stay with the students until they entered the building and then to pick up the buzz around the Court. Thanks to Dominick and the boy who left, I might get in.

After waiting another hour or so on the sidewalk, security guards brought us up a few steps to a plaza at the foot of the

main staircase. Dominick pointed to the frieze above and identified the stone figures: "That one is Moses, there's Confucius,
and the other one is Solon." A few of the students tossed remarks about the case back and forth, still engaged in amiable
argument after the long night on the sidewalk. However the
case turned out, I found myself thinking, Thomas Jefferson
would have been pleased to see these young people debating on
the steps of the nation's high tribunal.

The guards began counting off the people waiting in line. Of
the forty or so seats available, the students got the first ten and
the writer they had taken under their wing got number eleven.

Inside, the Supreme Court chamber evoked a Roman temple.
Fluted marble columns rose on both sidewalls and a huge crim-
son curtain hung behind the black-robed justices. To one side of
the elevated bench where the justices sat, the media section was
packed. The mahogany benches in the spectator area were filled
with observers who had some connection to the case or some
other entrée. I sat with the students and the other general-
admission guests in the very back, on cushionless bentwood
chairs of the sort you might find stored away in the basement of
a YMCA. Ushers and marshals controlled every movement in
the crowded courtroom. A secret service agent roamed our area
of the chamber, one hand holding his suit jacket slightly open.

The oral arguments began with the U.S. solicitor general
making the case for leaving the Pledge as it is. Then came Michael
Newdow, who had brought the original suit. An emergency-room
physician with a law degree but little courtroom experience, he
argued as his own advocate. Newdow put on a crackling perfor-
mance, methodically building his case and parrying challenges
from the justices. ("This reviewer gives him five stars," Dahlia
Lithwick later wrote in *Slate*. "He may still lose this appeal, but
he absolutely won the day.")

Nearly all of the justices offered different personal points of
view. For example, Justice Ruth Bader Ginsburg pointed out

that Newdow's daughter had the option of not saying the Pledge. Newdow countered by saying that just holding the ritual was coercive (which, incidentally, was a point agreed upon in the Ninth Circuit decision).

Justice David Souter felt that the term "under God" was expressed in such a rote manner that it had little true meaning anymore and was "too tepid, so diluted, so far from compulsory prayer that it is beneath the Constitutional radar." Justice John Paul Stevens mused similarly when he questioned whether "under God" had the same meaning and importance of impact as it had when it was first introduced into the Pledge.

Chief Justice William Rehnquist said he didn't think the Pledge sounded like a prayer. Newdow agreed, but pointed out that the Ten Commandments were not prayers, yet the Supreme Court had ruled that they had no place in public schools. Newdow also pointed out that in the Bush brief, Bush himself said the Pledge constitutes a prayer. Chief Justice Rehnquist responded by saying, "Well, but he— We certainly don't take him as the final authority on this." That remark prompted laughter from the crowd.

The justices also expressed concern that if "under God" was unconstitutional, then other forms of government recognition of God, as in, for example, "In God We Trust," would also be unconstitutional. As an atheist, Newdow couldn't have agreed more and, in fact, would have desired that all references to God be removed from government ceremonies, slogans, and coinage. (Newdow would later head a group that unsuccessfully sued to remove all religious references during the inauguration ceremonies for Barack Obama.)

At one point, Newdow even trumped Chief Justice William Rehnquist. Newdow contended that adding "under God" had a divisive effect on the nation, separating unbelievers from theists. Rehnquist asked Newdow what the tally had been in the 1954 vote to adopt the "under God" phrase.

"It was apparently unanimous," said Newdow. "There was no objection. . . ."

"Well, that doesn't sound divisive," Rehnquist responded with a hint of smugness.

There was a titter in the gallery.

"That's only because no atheist can get elected to public office," Newdow countered. The gallery erupted in laughter and applause. Rehnquist reddened.

"The courtroom will be cleared if there's any more clapping," he sputtered.

After the hearing, on the plaza in front of the Court, reporters crowded around Newdow. On the sidewalk below, free expression reigned. Demonstrators with signs that read "One Nation Under God" faced others carrying placards that said "Don't Make Religion a Condition of Patriotism" and "Hi, Mom, I'm an atheist!"

Three months later, on June 14, 2004, Flag Day (the second such Pledge decision handed down on Flag Day), the Supreme Court issued a ruling that overturned the Ninth Circuit decision on technical grounds. The opinion said Newdow lacked the legal standing to file a complaint in the first place because his daughter's mother, who never married Newdow, had controlling custody of the child. Although the effect was to preserve the "under God" Pledge, the finding sidestepped the basic question as to whether public school recitations of the 1954 text violated separation of church and state.

Three justices dissented for different reasons and each wrote their own opinion. Each, however, believed that the phrase "under God" was Constitutional.

Reactions to the decision were, of course, split between the two competing camps.

Newdow and his supporters were especially outraged with the Court's conclusion that he had no right to raise a question about how his child was treated in school. "I'm a father," said

Newdow, "and I have a right to make decisions for my child. I wonder, if she were being hit in the head with a 2-by-4 in school, would the Court also say I have no right to object? It just doesn't make sense."

Supporters of an unchanged Pledge were relieved to have dodged a bullet, but also disappointed that the matter was not settled definitively. As a *Boston Herald* columnist put it, "As victories go, it was a shallow one, but at least the U.S. Supreme Court reached the right conclusion in telling Michael Newdow . . . to take a hike."

As a result of the Supreme Court's action, the previous ruling in the Ninth Circuit court was reversed as a procedural matter, meaning that "under God" remained in the Pledge in all the states in the Ninth Circuit.

Newdow himself proclaimed that there were "fellow atheists standing in the wings." And indeed, following Newdow's defeat, other groups and individuals have attempted to bring the same issue before the court. They have targeted school districts within the purview of the U.S. Court of Appeals Ninth Circuit. By focusing on this geographic area, the strategy is, of course, that if the case gets to the Appeals Court level that arguments against the Pledge will receive the same positive reaction that was expressed in the majority decision in the Newdow case that pressed the review on up to the Supreme Court. That majority decision said, in part: "A profession that we are a nation 'under God' is identical, for Establishment Clause purposes, to a profession that we are a nation 'under Jesus,' a nation 'under Vishnu,' a nation 'under Zeus,' or a nation 'under no god,' because none of these professions can be neutral with respect to religion."

Clearly the Supreme Court has not been in any mood to make such a similar declaration. But that doesn't mean that it wouldn't at some time in the future. Those opposing the wording of the Pledge know this. They realize the only way to hit at the right moment is to keep the issue alive and circulating through the court system.

At the same time, politicians, gazing on Pledge popularity polls among voters, are already armed with legislative weapons to protect the Pledge as it stands. While no specific Constitutional amendment action has gotten very far, a congressional bill dubbed the Pledge Protection Act of 2005 sought to limit the powers of federal courts on any issue dealing with changes to the Pledge. This bill, as written, would prohibit federal courts, other than territorial courts, the Superior Court of the District of Columbia, and the District of Columbia Court of Appeals, from hearing or deciding cases questioning interpretation or Constitutional validity of the Pledge. In addition, it prohibits the Supreme Court from accepting appeals from *any* court on the issue. The legality of this act itself was questioned since Article 3 of the Constitution specifically ensures that federal judges are insulated from the political pressures governing members of the other two branches of government—legislative and executive. Ignoring that, however, the bill passed in Congress by a vote of 260 to 167. It was sent on to the Senate where it withered away in the Senate's Judicial Committee without ever being brought to a vote.

Although this particular bill is effectively dead, a spokesperson for one of the sponsors of the bill said, "It accomplished what we hoped for. The courts have not tried anything since."

If they do, there is plenty of precedent to suggest that politicians will react to public support of the Pledge by finding new ways of securing the oath's place as one of the touchstones of American political life. But the issue is certain to be litigated again and perhaps eventually to find its way once more to the Supreme Court. If so, whichever way the high tribunal decides, Americans will go on arguing about it long afterward.

12. THE ROLE OF THE PLEDGE TODAY

After more than a century and a quarter, the Pledge of Allegiance continues to exercise a profound and powerful influence over Americans. Incredibly, the many political battles and legal trials have not really altered it.

On the contrary, the periodic eruption of wrangling over the Pledge, its wording, its constitutionality, and its meaning, have helped shape Americans' view of themselves, sometimes to the left and sometimes to the right, without having sent Bellamy's oath to the dustbin of history or relegated it to the status of historical footnote. In fact, it has become something of a national Rorschach test, constantly revealing what it means to be an American. Like the Constitution, though with far fewer words, the Pledge is a "living" document, one whose identity is bound up with vigorous discussion, interpretation, and struggle. If combined with its continued popularity—recited more often than any other document of national identity—its longevity makes the Pledge seem almost like a "founding" document of the American experiment.

In this sense, the Pledge is both a timeless reaffirmation of basic shared principles and a shared ritual, like the singing of the National Anthem or voting on election day. Recitation as part of a group makes one part of something larger, but what is that "something"? If it is the idea of liberty, then why should we say it? And shouldn't we be free to reject it? After all, we don't *require* the singing of the Anthem—or even voting. How did the Pledge rise to status of Commandment?

The answer to that, as we've seen, is not so simple. At the heart of the American experiment is change and reinvention, such as the "living" Constitution, subject to reinterpretation. Yes, we are a nation of laws, but we are also a nation that believes firmly in the people's ability to change those laws—at their will.

Thus Governor Michael Dukakis vetoed a Massachusetts bill requiring teachers to lead classes in the Pledge of Allegiance and "paid dearly for it in his presidential campaign," as William Safire wrote in 2004. Taking on the Pledge is akin to spitting on the flag. What Dukakis did, as the George H. W. Bush campaign was more than happy to point out, was insult the flag, which is America. Dukakis gamely tried to argue that he was doing his patriotic duty, upholding the Constitution, but it didn't wash. The Pledge was as American as apple pie, maybe more so. And it had the advantage of brevity, the ring of a jingle—"See the USA, in a Chevrolet." It is conceivable that, as with the Chevy, we will remember the Pledge long after the flag and the republic for which it stands disappear.

For the moment, however, the flag, the Pledge, and the Republic survive. In fact, over the last decade, in part because of the events of September 11, 2001, the Pledge has become more prominent in schools than ever. The *Christian Science Monitor* reports that "since 9/11 more state and town laws actually require students to say the Pledge of Allegiance than ever." In 2004, Safire counted forty-two states with mandatory recitation laws.

For some, reciting the Pledge in school is what makes it, well, a school. Like show-and-tell, the Pledge belongs to time-honored primary education traditions. And this is a testament to Bellamy's genius: if you get school participation, you get lifelong learners. Habits of patriotism are set early. And if they are set in school, they endure.

It will thus be interesting to watch the Pledge as we reinvent and remake our school system. In a recent dispute over the virtues of homeschooling, for instance, a *Washington Post* editorial, "Parent Says Some Things Can't Be Taught at Home," prompted one traditional public school mother to write that her son in kindergarten was "learning to be part of [a] group, raise his hand to be heard, say the Pledge of Allegiance, wait quietly during a moment of silence and so much more." Can't do that at home.

Or can you? Some homeschooling parents (and there are now over a million in the United States, and the number is growing as online learning takes off), recognizing that the Pledge offers something irreplaceable, do recite it at home. "Each morning when it's time to go to school," reported the *Pasco* (Washington) *Times,* "the Seal children gather around the dining room table. Their mother leads them in morning prayers and the Pledge of Allegiance. Then the studies begin promptly at 8 a.m." So deep is our cultural association of the Pledge and school, that recitation of the words can have the effect of turning a dining room into a classroom. But how enforceable is it? Principals can peek into classrooms to make sure their teachers and students are conforming. Who will be looking into our dining rooms? Will the Pledge disappear in the same manner that it took hold?

Let's recall for a moment that when the editors of the *Youth's Companion* first hatched the idea of a celebration of America's founder, Christopher Columbus, they promoted the quadracentennial as a celebration of American schooling itself. A brilliant marketing strategy—what member of Congress would oppose schoolchildren reciting a patriotic oath?—such joining of the Pledge and schools also placed patriotism at the heart of public education at a time when public education was still a remarkably decentralized institution. (New York State, for instance, at the beginning of the twentieth century, had ten thousand autonomous school districts; today, with ten times the population, it has a little more than seven hundred. America's attachment to state and local autonomy is a serious one. Though today, our public school system seems "national" in scope and we are debating "national standards," we should recall that Thomas Jefferson's proposal for a "Bill for the More General Diffusion of Knowledge" as part of the revision of Virginia's laws in 1779 was largely defeated. "Despite his distrust of central authority," writes E. D. Hirsch, "Jefferson encouraged the devising of a common curriculum in order that 'the great mass of the people' should be taught not just the elements of reading, writing, and arithmetic, but also that 'their memories may here be stored with the most useful facts from Grecian, Roman, European, and American history,' as well as 'the first elements of morality.'"

And though Bellamy managed to gather a nationwide consensus for his Pledge, there were still plenty of members of Congress who were adamant about the federal government *not* paying for it. And we can gain a better appreciation of Bellamy's feat knowing how autonomous the thousands of schools in the United States were. It was the beginning of the creation of a national identity for the industrial age, at its most basic level: through the nation's children. And Bellamy offered just twenty-three words; an amazingly easy way to patriotism.*

With the exponential growth of homeschooling and its kissing cousin online learning, things could change dramatically for our Pledge.† But for now millions of American children, standing in

---

*It should also be noted that this was the same era when Catholics decided to start their public school system. In fact, the 1884 Baltimore conclave of Bishops ordered all American parishes to start a school. It proved an amazing unifier for Catholics: by the 1960s not only did Catholics educate one out of every eight American children, but they had helped enable the election of the country's first Catholic president, John F. Kennedy. And as we have already seen, Catholics were no slouches in the patriotism department: American flags, to this day, fly right alongside the Vatican flag in their classrooms (and churches).

†According to the National Center for Education Statistics, between 1999 and 2003 the number of homeschooled children increased from around 850,000 to roughly 1.1 million, a 29 percent jump in four years. Some people in the movement believe that the number is now as high as 2.5 million. We also now have a North American Council for Online Learning (NACOL), which reports a hectic pace of growth in the online education world: in 2000, there were 50,000 full- or part-time enrollments; in

classrooms across the country and as yet unacquainted with words like "allegiance" and "indivisible" are still repeating the phrases. It is one of the first extended quotations a child will learn—and remember for life. So ingrained from childhood is it that those of us who haven't recited the Pledge in years can pull it up from some primal memory cortex. Not long ago, a thirty-eight-year-old man who had been in a coma for six years miraculously awoke. His first words were "I love you, Mommy" and later, the first sixteen words of the Pledge of Allegiance: "I pledge allegiance to the flag of the United States of America and to the republic—." Was it significant that the man stopped before "under God"? Or was it, as the doctors said, a "medical miracle," not a religious one?

If the Pledge is intrinsically bound up with school, it is not merely for its educational properties or to teach grammatical or civic literacy. More important, the words recited at the beginning of a school day serve a ritual function. Like the National Anthem before a ball game, the words of the Pledge form a moment outside mundane time, demarking one part of the day from another. It signals a ritual start, and in that it gains power beyond the meaning of its words.

The Pledge does not end with grade school. Throughout the country, in city councils, state legislatures, meetings of benevolent associations such as the Rotary Club or the Kiwanis, patriotic groups such as the Veterans of Foreign Wars, or DAR, and Boy and Girl Scouts, the U.S. Congress, at the start of political conventions the Pledge of Allegiance is the beginning of business. The business of America: with liberty and justice for all.

And for both children and adults recitation of the Pledge is also more than just a starting gun to a hectic day or a meeting;

2005, there were 500,000; by 2007, it was a million. The growth of online learning enrollment in the last ten years, according to *Forbes* magazine, has been 30 percent annually, which is why the business magazine estimated that the market was worth $300 million in 2008.

it is a "community building" exercise, a momentary "coming together" before we pursue the individual liberties the Pledge confirms. The recitation of the Pledge—a pledge to the flag, after all—confirms our membership in a group, a "republic for which it stands," and to the smaller group of the classroom or the assembly floor. We gain power in a group, which is the seat of nationalism, a country coming together. Aren't we stronger for it as a nation? The schoolchildren who chant the Pledge together are learning their first civics lesson: participation. And while there are patriots who recite the Pledge by themselves— and it's too early in the Internet era to know its impact on our gathering rituals—the oath remains, at bottom, a communal mantra.

Whether this participation can or should be coerced is probably the only question that remains unanswered—and is, most likely, unanswerable. Most Americans would agree that the Pledge is a wonderful summation of American values; many believe, though, that its mandatory recitation undermines those values. That question promises to be an ongoing, possibly endless, dialogue, and no doubt our Supreme Court will be called on to make another judgment call, just as presidential candidates, depending on the temper of the times, will undoubtedly continue to wrap themselves in the flag—and its Pledge.

In the meantime, like the National Anthem, the flag, and the bald eagle, the Pledge belongs to the country's collection of patriotic symbols, enjoying solid public approval ratings. According to a 2008 Gallup Poll, 77 percent of Americans feel that children should be expected to recite the Pledge in school every morning. (There is some partisanship in this number: 89 percent of Republicans want it recited, but only 62 percent of Democrats do.)

But what is patriotism? What is its function? How do we come by it? In order to answer those questions, it is helpful to reconsider for a moment the recent history of the use of the

Pledge in our politics, during which, it's safe to say, both the best and worst of patriotic impulses were on display. We can, as the aphorism has it, "wrap" ourselves in the flag, as a way to protect us from the elements or shield us from criticism—or prevent us from answering the tough questions.

So it was in 1964 when Barry Goldwater's political commercial featured schoolchildren reciting the pledge intercut with Soviet leader Nikita Khrushchev threatening to destroy America. Khrushchev complained that his "We will bury you" quote was often taken out of context, but those protests mattered little in the frenzy of an American presidential campaign.

Twenty-four years later, during the 1988 presidential campaign, it was Democratic Party nominee Michael Dukakis who found himself trying to explain why he had vetoed a Pledge recitation law in 1977 when he was governor of Massachusetts. Dukakis rightly pointed out that the Supreme Court had, in the 1943 *Barnette* decision, struck down enforced recitation laws. "A fired-up Mr. Dukakis responded that Mr. Bush wasn't fit to be President if he couldn't understand the Constitution," reported *The New York Times*. "Mr. Bush replied that he understood the Constitution but that the Massachusetts bill had never been legally tested; had he been governor, he would have signed it and let the Supreme Court decide." Game, set, match.

The Pledge wins. The popular actor Charlton Heston, who joined Bush at campaign rallies, would lead audiences in recitations of the Pledge. Democrats gamely fought back, having Garrison Keillor, "the homespun humorist," as the *Times* called him, lead the Pledge at the Democratic convention. Mr. Bush ended his GOP acceptance speech with the Pledge. "Everyone seems to be trying to out-pledge everyone else," said the *Times,* which went on to opine, "It's silly. The Pledge expresses noble sentiments and celebrates shared values. But the Pledge is not the issue. The issue is whether the Pledge can be required. It does nothing to elevate the level of political discourse to turn a

complex Constitutional question into a litmus test of patriotism—
or of how to vote in November."

In one of their more heated exchanges, during a televised
debate in late September of 1988, Bush was asked by a ques-
tioner about his Pledge attacks on Dukakis. "I think I am more
in touch with the mainstream of America," the vice president
replied. "I hope people don't think I am questioning his patriotism. I am questioning his judgment."

Dukakis shot back, "Of course he is questioning my patriotism and I resent it."

But Dukakis's indignation proved ineffective against the
GOP's caricature of him, and Bush was right about being in better touch with mainstream America, which loved the Pledge—
probably more than the Constitution, whose Amendment
"freedoms" have always served more to protect minorities than
buttress the mainstream. In any case, the Pledge issue stuck and
Bush went on to win in a landslide victory.

The lesson was lost on no one. Both the House of Representatives and the Senate subsequently instituted a recitation of the
Pledge before opening their sessions, and as Richard Ellis has
pointed out, "The Pledge had become the third rail of politics,"
and the nation demanded, and continues to demand that its office seekers pass the "patriotism test."

If this political jockeying seems to confirm Samuel Johnson's
quip that "patriotism is the last refuge of a scoundrel," more
recent events offer a much muted picture.

The events of September 11, 2001, and the years since have
marked a turning point in the history and cultural relevance of
the Pledge. The spontaneous rise of patriotism after 9/11 combined with Michael Newdow's "under God" lawsuit, created,
as it were, a perfect storm for the Pledge. But overnight the
context had changed.

For the fifty years prior to the attacks on the World Trade
Center, the Pledge was seen as a bulwark to communism. The

addition of "under God" to the text of the Pledge, at the height of McCarthyism, was intended to provide a counterpoint to the "Godlessness" of our Russian enemies. After the Berlin Wall and the Soviet Union, however, the Pledge remained locked in the Cold War vortex. Thus it was that only a few months before 9/11, when Virginia state senator Warren E. Barry saw his Pledge mandate proposal being watered down by colleagues, he called them "spineless pinkos."

Almost overnight, after 9/11, the anti-Communist rhetoric that surrounded the conflict over the Pledge ended, and in the months that followed, the flag and the Pledge were framed once again by the rhetoric and images of a "hot" war, not a cold one. The image of the three firefighters raising the flag at ground zero became *the* iconic image of the tragedy and of American resilience in the face of adversity—and, not unnoticed, reminded the country of the courage of the Marines at Iwo Jima during World War II. A powerful and spontaneous movement to recite the Pledge sprang up nationwide, reminding us again of Bellamy's genius in creating what can only be called one of the best jingles of jingoism ever written.

As has often been the case with the Pledge, this new patriotism made itself felt first and foremost in the schools. There, patriotic symbols appeared with such suddenness and in such numbers that it almost appeared as if the nation was trying to erase the sickening images of the destroyed New York City skyscrapers, the hole in the Pennsylvania field (that saved the nation's Capitol), and the huge hole torn in the side of the Pentagon. Reported Kevin Sack in *The New York Times:*

> As a surge of patriotism has washed over the country in the wake of the terrorist attacks, nowhere has the revival been more omnipresent than in schools. Hallways and classrooms have been decorated with bunting and posters of Uncle Sam. Hundreds of thousands

of dollars have been raised for relief efforts through penny drives and bake sales. Blood drives have been held on campuses. Flags are showing up on clothing, book bags and lockers. . . . Schools that had mothballed the Pledge of Allegiance, like Batavia (Pa.) High School, have dusted it off, and those that had left its use up to teachers have made it mandatory. Celebration USA Inc., a civic group based in Orange County, Calif., hopes to synchronize a nationwide school recitation of the pledge at 2 p.m. Eastern time on Oct. 12. Teachers and principals report that once slouching students now stand at rapt attention and virtually shout a pledge they used to mumble. "You can actually hear people say the Pledge now," said Cedric E. Brown, the student council president at Jonesboro High, about 20 miles south of Atlanta.

In New York City, the site of the tragedy, the Board of Education passed a resolution, by a unanimous vote, one month after the attacks, to require that the Pledge be said (though it did not mandate participation in the recitation) at all public schools every morning and at every schoolwide function. In fact, the resolution was almost identical to one already on the books, but which had been routinely ignored, according to many observers, since the end of the Vietnam War.

Nevertheless, over the course of the following year, similar measures were adopted in Tennessee, Illinois, Montana, New Hampshire, and Pennsylvania. The vote in the Pennsylvania House was 200 to 1. In places where such laws already existed, they took on a new meaning. In Virginia, State Senator Barry, who had chided committee members as "pinkos," now found his bill to have been exceedingly "timely." Before 9/11 his Pledge law was met by criticism, indifference, and boycott in many

Virginia schools. Afterward, no one objected. "Before the terrorist attacks, everyone just sort of stayed in their seats," said Katherine Dodson, a fifteen-year-old sophomore at H.B. Woodlawn school in Arlington, just across the river from the Pentagon. "No one even acknowledged the fact that we were supposed to be saying the Pledge. It's hard for a school to come together—the Pledge of Allegiance was the last thing I thought our school would come together and do."

The states had their say; so did the federal government. On September 13, 2001, President George W. Bush, and former presidents Clinton, Bush, and Carter, recited the Pledge together at the National Cathedral in Washington, D.C. And less than a month after the tragedy, Education Secretary Rod Paige sent letters to 100,000 schools recommending a simultaneous recitation of the Pledge. It was an idea, he later said, he got from a teacher.

Indeed, a "Pledge Across America" initiative had begun more than a decade earlier, in the years preceding the largely ignored centennial of the Pledge in 1992, and was spearheaded by a California substitute teacher named Paula Burton. Burton hatched the centennial idea after writing "indivisible" on the blackboard of her fifth-grade classroom and hearing students say that it meant "can't be seen." (Humorist Art Buchwald was asked if he was aware of the Pledge's centennial and he quipped, "Not only was I aware of it, I was there.")

And Rome, New York, was not ignorant of the anniversary made famous by its favorite son. "Pride and affection were evident as an estimated 2,000 people turned out to honor both the centennial of the Pledge of Allegiance and the memory of its author," began a story in the *Rome Daily Sentinel*. New York's first lady, Matilda Cuomo, was at Fort Stanwix National Monument, and camera crews for two of the three national broadcast networks had been in town to film segments for their morning shows. "Pride in country doesn't play well in some communities," said the pastor of the local Baptist church, capturing the mood of the country better than he may have intended, "but in Rome it's a beautiful symphony." It was also the First Day of Issue for a Pledge postage stamp (first-class mail was then 29 cents).

In the ebb and flow of political iconography, the Pledge was at a low-tide moment in 1992, a year of relative peace and prosperity in the United States (it was the year in which Bosnia and Herzegovina seceded from Yugoslavia, Quebec voters decided to stay with Canada, John Gotti was convicted of thirteen counts of racketeering, Mike Tyson was found guilty of rape, and Johnny Carson left the *Tonight Show*. Oh, yes, and Bill Clinton defeated George Bush for president that year—and the Pledge played no part in it).

By October 2001, of course, the nation was at war. And there was no lack of enthusiasm for a patriotic act.

"Our flag is a symbol for all Americans that we are protected from violence and terrorism," Secretary of Education Paige wrote to the nation's public school leaders. "It is important for teachers to display that freedom and patriotism by focusing on the flag."

No doubt September 11 had changed the equation. What at its worst had been a cynical ploy of partisan politics became, in the hour of crisis, a symbol of real unity. The group activity of reciting the Pledge reaffirmed founding principles that were suddenly threatened. "I think it is important that at a time like this we all focus on the positive," Principal Janet Foster, of Fox Mill Elementary School in Herndon, Virginia, said after the "Pledge across America" event. "I want these children to feel safe, that we are all in this together. The Pledge is another way of showing how we feel as a group."

Eventually the super-patriotism of September 11 relaxed, and recitations of the Pledge were less monitored. The further the country moved away from the emergency, the more comfortable it became with loosening mandates on the recitation of the national oath. Even by the end of November of 2001, the District 3 school board in New York City, ground zero for 9/11, had decided that its thirty-one schools should decide on their own to say the Pledge in the morning. "Requiring students to blindly repeat the Pledge is no different than the Taliban requiring children to memorize the Koran and repeat it by rote, without understanding why or what they are saying," said Larry Sauer, the board member behind the move.

Only in America!

Barely two months after the most lethal attack on the United States since Pearl Harbor and already someone was comparing the victim to the aggressor.

And by July of 2003 a federal judge struck down a law requiring Pennsylvania school students to recite the Pledge. U.S. District Judge Robert F. Kelly said the law was an improper attempt to circumvent *Barnette,* the Supreme Court's opinion issued sixty years earlier.

What really brought to an end the period of spontaneous patriotism was the war on terror itself. To the extent that the Pledge represents fealty to national purpose and policy, as much as to core principles, the diminished enthusiasm for saying it represented America's increasing ambivalence to the Bush war. (A loss of enthusiasm for the Pledge followed Vietnam as well.) As communal grieving gave way to a controversial war, the solidarity around the Pledge could not last.

In late September 2001, barely three weeks after the fall of the World Trade Center, a day after the start of Operation Enduring Freedom in Afghanistan, a Wisconsin school district banned a mandated recitation of the Pledge. Even in a media jam-packed with news of vital and historic impact, the Pledge decision would come to command national attention as television stations, newspapers, magazines, Matt Drudge, and Rush Limbaugh, rushed to heap scorn on the school board as unpatriotic. And several weeks later, on October 15, the board met to reconsider and was met by an audience of twelve hundred who shouted the Pledge, and followed it up with a chant of "USA! USA! USA!" By a vote of 6 to 1, the board overturned its earlier decision.

The shift from the use of the Pledge as a unifying force immediately after 9/11 to its familiar incarnation as a battering ram against woolly-headed "liberals" and the "cultural elite" was complete within six months. But it was half a year in which much had transpired. Indeed, the shift in the role of the Pledge corresponded to a transformation in the national mood as the country swung from mourning to a demand for justice, even vengeance.

This sentiment was never entirely lacking after the attacks on the World Trade Center. On September 20, President Bush famously told a joint session of Congress: "Either you are with us or you are with the terrorists." His assertion in his State of the Union address on January 29, 2002, that there existed an "axis of evil" was another landmark on the road to full-fledged war.

But if much of the country was taking its cues from the tone of the president, the event that completely polarized opinions around the Pledge was the decision by the Ninth Circuit Court of Appeals in June 2002, agreeing with plaintiff Michael Newdow who complained that the Pledge was unconstitutional.

Only in America.

The proximity in time of the attack on the World Trade Center and the finding that the Pledge was unconstitutional, barely nine months apart, was uncanny. The two events, one inspiring instinctual and voluntary patriotism and the second challenging such patriotism, displayed an almost schizophrenic American temperament. Either that, or it was a sign that we were returning to the normalcy of the democratic (arguing) landscape. Still, the reaction to the court verdict was extraordinarily lopsided. The president called the decision "ridiculous."

The Senate voted unanimously to condemn the decision. The House Majority whip, Trent Lott (R.-Miss.), called it "absurd." The Senate Majority leader, Tom Daschle (D.-S. Dak.), lambasted it as "just nuts."

Although America has a long history of arguing over religious freedom, the Ninth Circuit court's decision brought the Pledge squarely into the "for us or against us" arena at a time when the president himself had said it. And few politicians, whatever their political stripe, were willing to argue against the oath, especially at a time of intense patriotism. It was not long after the U.S. Supreme Court's ruling in the Newdow case that the 2008 presidential contest began in earnest, and the rumor began to circulate that Senator Barack Obama (D.-Ill.) refused to say the Pledge. "Barack Obama, born in Africa, is a possibly gay Muslim racist who refuses to recite the Pledge of Allegiance," according to a *Washington Post* summary of the rumors.

These slurs stood in stark contrast to Obama's Democratic opponent for the nomination, Senator Hillary Clinton, who had attacked the 2002 Ninth Circuit court decision in 2008, saying "I believe the court misinterpreted the intent of the framers of the Constitution and instead undermined one of the bedrocks of our democracy, that we are indeed, 'one nation under God,'" and then, to much applause, reiterated her belief that "every American child should start the day saying the Pledge of Allegiance."

Obama's patriotism continued to be an issue even after he secured his party's nomination, though this was perhaps a predictable response to the fact that his Republican opponent, Senator John McCain, was a war hero and former POW who had pledged allegiance to a makeshift flag while imprisoned in North Vietnam.

Twenty-four years after the Dukakis defeat, however, Obama understood the stakes and refused to be tarred with the same brush. Utilizing the Internet, he created a website, fightthesmears.com, beating back the rumors and posting a video of himself leading the Senate in the Pledge. As we know, he won.

In the end, however, the Pledge faces an uncertain future. The failure of the Supreme Court to resolve the "under God" question leaves a lingering doubt about that phrase's constitutionality. And a new twist to the critique came in 2005 when the Virginia Supreme Court had to declare that the Pledge, despite "under God," was not a prayer. Understandably, a group of thirty-two Christian and Jewish clergy objected, claiming that if children are supposed to say the phrase without meaning it as a religious affirmation, "then every day, the government asks millions of schoolchildren to take the name of the Lord in vain."

Francis Bellamy, the former minister, would have appreciated the theological conundrums that his Pledge had occasioned, though his Pledge was decidedly not religious. And one suspects that had he been presented with "under God" on that hot summer night in 1892, by some muse, or an editor, he would have rejected it. His son, David Bellamy, told Congressman Kenneth Keating during the 1953 debate that he objected to the rewriting. And Bellamy's great-granddaughter, Sally Wright, weighed in in 2002, replying to a story in *The New York Times* by Arthur Schlesinger, Jr.:

> *To the Editor:*
> *Re "When Patriotism Wasn't Religious," by Arthur Schlesinger Jr. (Op-Ed, July 7):*
> *My great-grandfather Francis Bellamy wrote the Pledge of Allegiance in 1892 for the widely read magazine* Youth's Companion. *A deeply religious man, he was also a strict believer in the separation of church and state, one who opposed parochial schools on the grounds that the state should educate its children. He intended the Pledge to be a unifying statement for those same children.*

> *By adding the phrase "under God" to the Pledge of*
> *Allegiance in 1954, Congress was attempting to distinguish*
> *the politics of the United States from godless Communism.*
> *Like other actions taken by Congress at that time, this change*
> *divided our nation further rather than uniting its citizens.*
>
> *As a regular churchgoer who has voted both Democratic*
> *and Republican, I believe that my great-grandfather got it*
> *right. A Pledge of Allegiance that does not include God*
> *invites the participation of more Americans.*
>
> SALLY WRIGHT
> *Pleasant Hill, Calif, July 7, 2002*

While the debate over forced recitation seemed a straightforward question about what a school can and cannot compel a child or teacher to do—or say—the God question is something else. It is embedded in the oath, as clearly and starkly as "indivisible," "the republic," and "liberty and justice." Even God-fearing and God-believing people are uncomfortable with it.

Does recitation of the Pledge signify tacit support for government policies? Does the "under God" clause signify allegiance to God as well as country? These questions remain unanswered—perhaps because there is no way to answer them. Nonetheless, the fact that the Pledge continues to be recited even as it is argued over does reveal certain characteristics of American life and beliefs, the most notable of which, perhaps, is a deeply felt insecurity. For at heart, the Pledge is a binding oath, meant to guarantee the fidelity of citizens to the republic. That could be why, besides its usage as starting ritual and a community builder in schools, legislatures, and meeting halls, it also finds its place in the induction of new citizens to the United States. A promise of loyalty. In 2008 alone, one million people were inducted as new citizens of the United States. For them the Pledge doesn't merely start the school day, or the day of government business; it starts, rather, the new life of being an American.

This use of the Pledge, as a "loyalty oath," echoes its origins in the midst of a historic wave of immigration, something akin to a national identity crisis. The nation needed to be reminded of its core values. But the fact that schoolchildren, legislators, and others still recite the Pledge on a regular basis may indicate an even deeper uncertainty. Here lies the fundamental paradox of the Pledge: it bespeaks both pride in a nation "with liberty and justice for all," but also suggests that without constant reaffirmation those principles would disappear.

Those who have been on the anti-Pledge side of the debate have often pointed out the schism. Hence Justice Robert Jackson's dissenting opinion in the 1943 *Gobitis* case:

> To believe that patriotism will not flourish if patriotic ceremonies are voluntary and spontaneous instead of a compulsory routine is to make an unflattering estimate of the appeal of our institutions to free minds.

Likewise, when Minnesota governor Jesse Ventura, the former professional wrestler and Navy SEAL, bravely vetoed a bill mandating recitation of the Pledge in 2002, he asserted that "patriotism comes from the heart. Patriotism is voluntary. It is a feeling of loyalty and allegiance that is the result of knowledge and belief."

After 125 years, if polls are to be believed, we remain a nation that feels more comfortable being safe than sorry—and perhaps in need of a reminder of what we "stand for." The Pledge continues to enjoy overwhelming support, as does the inclusion of the "under God" clause. As former presidential speechwriter Peggy Noonan put it, "I've concluded the Pledge of Allegiance is about as perfect as imperfect humans could devise. It pledges loyalty and love to a symbol of our nation, the nation itself, and its Constitutional form; it asserts unbreakable unity, acknowledges

God, and aspires, at the end, to democratic perfection. Pretty good! And in only 31 words."

The question remains: are twenty-three words better? Judge, dear reader, for yourself:

> I pledge allegiance to the flag of the United States
> of America, and to the republic for which it stands,
> one nation, under God, indivisible, with liberty and
> justice for all.

Or

> I pledge allegiance to my flag, and to the republic
> for which it stands, one nation, indivisible, with
> liberty and justice for all.

The debate over the Pledge of Allegiance will no doubt continue—at least, we should hope that it does. For it is in that quarrel and uncensored debate that we find the essence of our democracy and the health of our republic.

BIBLIOGRAPHY

There are literally thousands of sources of information for the story of the Pledge of Allegiance, and hundreds were accessed to write this history. The bibliography below includes both published and unpublished resources, ranging from broad histories of nineteenth- and twentieth-century America to intricate stories of the Bellamy family and the *Youth's Companion*. To do a proper accounting of the Pledge as it was lived and debated over the last 120 years, we need to know something about the Civil War and its aftermath, about the debate over public schools, the meaning of the Gilded Age, and the arguments about socialism, as well as what Henry Luce, founder of *Time* magazine, called "the American century," the one just passed, and the central role of the Pledge in our evolving understanding of the First Amendment and the group that proved to be one of its great defenders. The fact that President Dwight Eisenhower was raised a Jehovah's Witness, the religious sect that fought against the mandatory recitation of the Pledge for several decades, and signed into law the most controversial rephrasing of the Pledge, is just one of the more fascinating parts of this history. And then there was 9/11.

The references below were all used in the writing of this book and provide a deep background for our story. They should be included in our acknowledgments since they provide a rich and profound record of fact and opinion about the Pledge of Allegiance and what it means to "the Republic for which it stands."

The reader may dip into any of them to be both enlightened and entertained.

Adams, Gridley. *So Proudly We Hail*. United States Flag Foundation, 1953.

American Press Association. "Columbus Day Page, No. 3," A full page (11x20), no date. Includes the "Address for Columbus Day" by "the Youth's Companion," "The Official Programme," the "Ode for Columbus Day" by Edna Dean Proctor, and "The President's Proclamation." Francis Julius Bellamy Papers (see Bellamy, Francis Julius, p.191).

Baer, John W. *The Pledge of Allegiance: A Centennial History, 1892–1992*. Annapolis, Md.: Free State Press, Inc., 1992. Partial availability online at http://oldtimeislands.org/pledge/pdgecho.htm . Downloaded January 2010. The book is cited in footnote number one in the written U.S. Supreme Court decision of *Elk Grove School District v. Michael Newdow*, June 14, 2004, available at http://www.law.cornell.edu/supct/html/02-1624.ZO.html#FN5. Downloaded January 2010.

———. *The Pledge of Allegiance: A Revised History and Analysis, 1892–2007*. Annapolis, Md.: Free State Press, Inc. Partial availability online at http://oldtimeislands.org/pledge/pdgecho.htm. Downloaded January 2010.

———. *The Pledge of Allegiance: A Short History*. Available at http://oldtimeislands.org/pledge/plege.htm. Downloaded January 2010.

Bailey, Diana L. *American Treasure: The Enduring Spirit of the DAR*. Marceline, Mo.: Walsworth Publishing Company, 2007.

Balch, George T. *Methods of Teaching Patriotism in the Public Schools*. New York: D. Van Nostrand, 1890.

Bellamy, David. *David Bellamy Papers*. Department of Rare Books, Special Collections and Preservation, Rush Rhees Library, University of Rochester, Rochester, New York. Date Range: 1890–1980. 3 boxes. The David Bellamy Papers are primarily concerned with the controversy surrounding the authorship of the Pledge. Ref. http://www.lib.rochester .edu/index.cfm?page=790. Downloaded January 2010.

Bellamy, Edward. *Looking Backward*. Boston: Picknar, 1888; reprint, New York: New American Library, Signet Classic, 1960.

Bellamy, Francis Julius. Francis Julius Bellamy Papers [FJBP]. Department of Rare Books, Special Collections and Preservation, Rush Rhees Library, University of Rochester, Rochester, New York. Date Range: 1890–2002. 6 boxes, 1 package. This collection is closely related to collection D.147, Bellamy (David) Papers, 1892–1980. Ref. http://www.lib.rochester .edu/index.cfm?page=1779. Downloaded January 2010. An index to the collection contents is available online.

———. Affidavit. State of New York, County of New York. August 13, 1923. Exhibit A is 11 pages, includes copy of "leaflet," "The Youth's Companion Flag Pledge."

———. Affidavit. State of New York, County of New York. August 30, 1923. 9 pages. Includes exhibits: letter from Francis Bellamy to C. E. Kelsey of the *Youth's Companion,* June 21, 1923 (3 pages); "second letter" from Perry Mason to Francis Bellamy, August 1, 1923 (1 page); "second letter" from Bellamy to "Mr. Kelsey," June 30, 1923 (2 pages); reply of Perry Mason company to Francis Bellamy, July 9, 1923 (1 page); "third letter" from Bellamy to "Mr. Kelsey," dated July 23, 1923 (7 pages); Bellamy was living, at the time, at 244 Central Park West, New York, N.Y.

———. Affidavit. State of New York, County of New York. September 1, 1923. Includes exhibits: letter from Harold Roberts, dated March 15, 1923; "To Whom It May Concern" letter from Mrs. Lue Stuart Wadsworth, dated April 28, 1923; letter from Mrs. Lue Stuart Wadsworth, dated July 8, 1923; letter from Mrs. Florence Buckllin Scott, wife of John Winfield Scott, July 15, 1923.

———. "The Address for Columbus Day: The Meaning of the

Four Centuries." A two-page printed sheet, "Supplement to Official Program," with "By Francis Bellamy" written by hand. Includes "The Address for Primary Schools (Simplified from the preceding.)" FJBP.

———. No title. No date. Five-page typescript summary of the National Public School Celebration. Handwritten initial at the end, "FB."

———. "State Supts. of Schools." A one-page typescript listing of the forty-nine state superintendents. No attribution.

———. "Dear Mr. Ford," April 18, 1892. Six-page typescript written letter to Daniel Ford, on letterhead of the National Columbian Public School Celebration. Bellamy asks permission to interview the "leading men in Washington."

———. Letter to the Honorable Sheldon Jackson, Washington, D.C., from the National Columbian Public School Celebration of October 12, 1892, Chairman's Office, The Youth's Companion Building, April 12, 1892. Signed by Francis Bellamy. A handwritten note at the top of the page says "Copy of letter to State Supts." At the top, in small print, is a quote: "Not only to interest the youth of the Country in the World's Columbian Exposition, but also to give to the American Public School a fitting prominence as the fruit of four centuries of American Life." Also, see letter to T. B. Stockwell (April 29, 1892), almost four pages long, beginning, "I wrote you on April 12th . . . , but I have not received your answer yet."

———. "To the Editor of The Inter Ocean, Chicago, Ill.," from the National Columbian Public School Celebration of October 12, 1892, Chairman's Office, The Youth's Companion Building, April 13, 1892. Handwritten note at the top of the page says, "Letter to the Metropolitan Press." Attached is a one-page "Statement to Editors," also signed by Bellamy, and a copy of "Message to the Public Schools of America."

———. "To the Editor of the American Teacher, Boston, Mass." from the National Columbian Public School Celebration of October 12, 1892, Chairman's Office, The Youth's Companion Building, April 20, 1892, signed by Francis Bellamy "for the Executive Committee." A handwritten note at the top of the page says "Copy of Personal letter to educational press."

Blumenthal, Sidney. *Pledging Allegiance: The Last Campaign of the Cold War.* New York: Harper Collins, 1990.

Boime, Albert. *The Unveiling of the National Icons: A Plea for Patriotic Iconoclasm in a Nationalist Era.* Cambridge University Press, 1998.

Boston *Herald.* "What Is Being Done: For Thirteen Millions. A Columbian Celebration for the Public Schools." March 31, 1892. A one-page facsimile, with the following introduction: "This perhaps can best be told in the story of the following Interview, recently held with the Chairman of the Executive Committee at the Instance of the Boston Herald. The Chairman, therefore, begs to be allowed to present the story in this form to the Honorable State Superintendents of Public Instruction." Interview with Francis Bellamy. FJBP.

Brandt, Nat. "To the Flag," *American Heritage: The Magazine of History,* June 1971.

Brinkley, Douglas, and Julie M. Fenster. *Parish Priest: Father Michael McGivney and American Catholicism.* New York: William Morrow Publishers, 2006.

Coopersmith, Jerome. "The Curious Case of the Unsigned Pledge," *Family Circle,* July 1970. This is the story of Margarette S. Miller, "a young girl [who] unraveled this famous American mystery."

Coulter, Ann. *Treason: Liberal Treachery from the Cold War to the War on Terrorism.* New York: Crown Forum, 2003.

Curtis, Michael Kent, ed. *The Constitution and the Flag.* New York: Garland, 1993.

Dewey, John. *Democracy and Education.* New York: Free Press, 1916.

Dombrowski, James. *The Early Days of Christian Socialism in America.* New York: Columbia University Press, 1936.

Dreier, Peter, and Dick Flacks. "Patriotism's Secret History," *The Nation,* June 3, 2002.

Duncan, D. E. *Calendar: Humanity's Epic Struggle to Determine a True and Accurate Year.* New York: Harper Perennial, 1999.

Eisler, Kim Isaac. *A Justice for All.* New York: Simon & Schuster, 1993.

Ellis, Richard J. *To the Flag: The Unlikely History of the Pledge of Allegiance.* Lawrence: University Press of Kansas, 2005.

Finn, Chester E., Jr. "Teaching Patriotism: An Educational Resource for America." *National Review Online,* December 6, 2001. Available at www.nationalreview.com/comment/comment-finnprint120601.html. Downloaded January 2010.

———. "Patriotism Revisited." *Center for Education Reform,* October 1, 2001. Available at http://www.edreform.com/Resources/Editorials/?Patriotism_Revisited&year=2001. Downloaded January 2010.

Forelle, Charles. "Time and Again, the Calendar Comes Up Short." *Wall Street Journal,* December 30, 2009. The calendar controversy continues.

Foster, Wallace. *A Patriotic Primer for the Little Citizen,* rev. and enl. Indianapolis: Levey Bros., 1898.

Frates, Chris. "High School Junior Suspended After Posting Anti-War Fliers." *Denver Post,* February 28, 2003.

Goldman, Emma. "Patriotism: A Menace to Liberty." In *Anarchism and Other Essays.* New York: Dover Books, 1969. Available at http://womenshistory.about.com/library/etext/bl_eg_an5_patriotism_menace_to_liberty.htm. Downloaded January 2010.

Grand Army of the Republic. *Journal of the Thirty-Ninth National Encampment of the Grand Army of the Republic.* Denver, Colorado, September 7 and 8, 1905. Boston: Griffith-Stillings Press. Available at http://books.google.com/books?id=WqH1b HilKDMC&pg=PA171&lpg=PA171&dq=Chief+Aide+in+ Charge+of+Military+Instruction+and+Patriotic+Education

+in+Schools,+Allan+Bakewell,&source=bl&ots=yys
5LOzBQo&sig=8zKNZ39Ws3doys3df7BAAPp9nhc&hl=
en&ei=W5xgS9HkA4b8lAeR_7zbCw&sa=X&oi=book_re
sult&ct=result&resnum=1&ved=oCAcQ6AEwAA#v=
onepage&q=the%20flag%20should%20be%20floated&f=
false. Downloaded January 2010. Reference here to flag
etiquette by Allan Blakewell.

Guenter, Scot. *The American Flag, 1777–1924.* Rutherford, N.J.:
Fairleigh Dickinson University Press, 1990.

Harris, Louise. *The Flag Over the School House.* C.A. Stephens
Collection, Brown University, Providence, R.I., 1971. Harris's book is a must-read for anyone interested in the story of
the Pledge because she reproduces dozens of original documents, including articles from *Youth's Companion,* whose rec-
ords were destroyed.

Hentoff, Nat. "The Patriotism Enforcers: Miseducating the
Young on Freedom." *Village Voice,* January 2–8, 2002.

Hirsch, E. D., Jr. *The Making of Americans: Democracy and Our
Schools.* New Haven, Conn.: Yale University Press, 2008.

———. *The Schools We Need: And Why We Don't Have Them.*
New York: Random House, 1996; reprinted New York: An-
chor Books, 1999.

Holzer, Harold, ed. *The Lincoln Anthology: Great Writers on His
Life and Legacy from 1860 to Now.* New York: The Library of
America, 1989.

Hunter, Ann Arnold. *A Century of Service: The Story of the DAR.*
Washington, D.C.: National Society Daughters of the American Revolution, 1991.

Jones, Jeffrey Owen. "The Pledge's Creator." *Smithsonian,* November 2003.

Kahn, E. J., Jr. "Three Cheers for the Blue, White, and Red."
The New Yorker, July 5, 1952.

Kaufman, Christopher. *Faith and Fraternalism.* New York: Harper
and Row, 1982. The story of the Knights of Columbus.

BIBLIOGRAPHY

Kaufmann, Bill. "The Bellamy Boys Pledge Allegiance." *American Enterprise,* October 1, 2002.

Kelly, Augustus H., and Emma Bates Harvey. *The Simmons Reading Books: Book Eight.* New York: Parker P. Simmons Co., Inc., 1914, 1917. This was a standard eighth-grade reading book used in schools at the beginning of the twentieth century. It is a collection of dozens of popular songs, poems, and essays.

Kovach, Bill. "Journalism and Patriotism." Talk given to the annual meeting of the Organization of News Ombudsmen, April 30, 2002. Available at www.newsombudsmen.org/kovach.html. Downloaded January 2010.

Kubal, Timothy. *Cultural Movements and Collective Memory: Christopher Columbus and the Rewriting of the National Origin Myth.* New York: Palgrave Macmillan, 2008.

Lapkoff, Shelley. *The Amazing History of the Pledge.* Available at http://www.historyofthepledge.com/. Downloaded January 2010. Lapkoff provides information on William Howell and Navesink.

Larson, Erik. *The Devil in the White City: Murder, Magic, and Madness at the Fair That Changed America.* New York: Crown, 2003.

Leepson, Marc. *Flag: An American Biography.* New York: Thomas Dunne Books, 2005.

Lerner, Michael. *The Left Hand of God: Taking Back Our Country from the Religious Right.* San Francisco: Harper, 2006.

Leuchtenburg, William E. *The Supreme Court Reborn: The Constitutional Revolution in the Age of Roosevelt.* New York: Oxford University Press, 1995.

Lipow, Arthur. *Authoritarian Socialism in America: Edward Bellamy and the Nationalist Movement.* Berkeley: University of California Press, 1982.

Manwaring, David R. *Render Unto Caesar: The Flag-Salute Controversy.* Chicago: University of Chicago Press, 1962.

Martin, Bill, and Michael Sampson. *I Pledge Allegiance.* Cambridge, Mass.: Candlewick Press, 2002. A children's book.

196

McCain, Senator John. "Why the Pledge of Allegiance." *Center for Education Reform.* October 1, 2001. Available at http://www.edreform.com/Resources/Editorials/?Why_the_Pledge_Of_Allegiance&year=2001. Downloaded January 2010.

McConnell, Stuart. *Glorious Contentment: The Grand Army of the Republic, 1865–1900.* Chapel Hill: University of North Carolina Press, 1992.

McPherson, James M., ed. *"To the Best of My Ability: The American Presidents."* London: DK Publishing, Inc., 2000; revised U.S. Edition, New York: DK Publishing, 2004.

Melrose, Massachusetts, "Notable Historic Houses." Phineas Upham House. Address: 255 Upham Street. Year built: 1703. "Interesting Facts: One of the members of the Upham family (James B. Upham) wrote the Pledge of Allegiance to the Flag in 1888. Also, the Phineas Upham House is listed on the National Historic Register. Available at http://www.cityofmelrose.org/Interns%2007/historichouses1.htm#Upham House. Downloaded January 2010.

Meyer, Adolphe E. *An Educational History of the American People.* New York: McGraw-Hill Book Company, Inc., 1957.

Meyer, Peter. "Mission Impossible: Can Catholic Schools Be Saved?" *Education Next,* Spring 2007.

Miller, Margarette S. *Twenty-Three Words.* Portsmouth, Va.: Printcraft Press, 1976.

Morgan, Arthur E. *Edward Bellamy.* New York: Columbia University Press, 1944.

Mott, Frank Luther. *A History of American Magazines, 1850–1865.* Cambridge, Mass.: Harvard University Press, 1938.

Moyer, G. "The Gregorian Calendar." *Scientific American,* May 1982.

Nasaw, David. *Schooled to Order: A Social History of Public Schooling in the United States.* New York, Oxford University Press, 1979; Oxford University Press paperback, 1981.

National Columbian Public School Celebration, Executive

Committee. "Department of Superintendence." FJBP. A one-page memo, "Suggestions for Campaign." No date. Executive Committee: Francis Bellamy, chairman, representing the *Youth's Companion,* Boston, Mass.; John W. Dickinson, secretary of Massachusetts Board of Education; Thomas B. Stockwell, commissioner of public schools of Rhode Island; W. R. Garrett, superintendent of public instruction of Tennessee; W. C. Hewitt, superintendent of Michigan educational exhibit at World's Fair.

———. "Message to the Public Schools of America," a printed page "first published March 31" and carrying the advisory, "This should be Printed in every Newspaper in the State." FJBP.

———. "Official Program, The National School Celebration of Columbus Day, October 21, 1892," 3 pages, no date. FJBP.

"Khrushchev Tirade Again Irks Envoys." *New York Times.* November 19, 1956.

"A Columbian Public School Celebration." *New York Tribune.* February 18, 1892. From one-page "Extract." FJBP. Includes "the full text of the Resolutions presented by Dr. W. T. Harris, U.S. Commissioner of Education."

Nussbaum, M., and J. Cohen. *For Love of Country: Debating the Limits of Patriotism.* Cambridge, Mass.: Beacon Press, 1996.

O'Leary, Cecilia Elizabeth. *To Die For: The Paradox of American Patriotism.* Princeton, N.J.: Princeton University Press, 1999.

Paul, Marilyn H. "I Pledge Allegiance . . ." *Prologue: Quarterly of the National Archives,* Winter 1992.

Penton, James M. *Apocalypse Delayed: The Story of Jehovah's Witnesses.* 2nd ed. Toronto: University of Toronto Press, 1997. First published in 1985.

Peters, Shawn Francis. *Judging Jehovah's Witnesses: Religious Persecution and the Dawn of the Rights Revolution.* Lawrence: University Press of Kansas, 2000.

Piscatelli, Jennifer. "Pledge of Allegiance." *Education Commission of the States,* 2003. Available at www.ecs.org/clearing house/47/20/4720.htm.

Ravitch, Diane. *Left Back: A Century of Failed School Reforms.* New York: Simon & Schuster, 2000.

———. "Teaching History in a Time of Terror." Center for Education Reform, October 1, 2001. Available at http://www.edreform.com/Resources/Editorials/?Teaching_History_in_a_Time_Of_Terror&year=2001. Downloaded January 2010.

Rubel, David, ed. *The Bedside Baccalaureate: A Handy Dandy Daily Cerebral Primer to Fill in the Gaps, Refresh Your Knowledge & Impress Yourself & Other Intellectuals.* New York: Sterling, 2008.

Salamida, Steven. "Spirit of Pledge Shines on Bellamy Day," *Rome* (New York) *Daily Sentinel,* September 8, 1992.

Schlesinger, Arthur M. *The Politics of Upheaval: The Age of Roosevelt, 1935–1936.* New York: Houghton Mifflin, 1960; New York: Mariner, 2003.

School Journal, The. "Who Originated Columbus School Day?" November 12, 1892. Page 436. The story is "signed" as by "Patriotism," and there is a 4-page typescript version of same story, with handwritten corrections. FJBP.

Sica, Morris G. "The School Flag Movement: Origin and Influence." *Social Education,* October 1990.

Strayer, Martha. *The D.A.R.: An Informal History.* Washington, D.C.: Public Affairs Press, 1958.

Swanson, June. *I Pledge Allegiance.* Minneapolis: Carolrhoda Books, 2002. This is a children's book. Pictures by Rick Hanson.

Time magazine. "Heroes: Upham Furled." May 29, 1939.

———. "We Will Bury You!" November 26, 1956.

Valeri, Mark. *Law and Providence in Joseph Bellamy's New England: The Origins of the New Divinity in Revolutionary America.* New York: Oxford University Press, 1994.

Wellner, Alison Stein, "The Perils of Patriotism." *American Demographics,* September 2002.

West, Cornel. *Democracy Matters: Winning the Fight Against Imperialism.* New York: Penguin, 2004.

Westheimer, Joel. *Pledging Allegiance: The Politics of Patriotism in America's Schools.* Foreword by Howard Zinn. Teaching for Social Justice Series. New York: Teachers College Press, 2007. Contributions in this book are from some of the nation's leading thinkers about education, including Diane Ravitch ("Celebrating America"), Charles Payne ("No Black in the Union Jack: The Ambivalent Patriotism of Black Americans"), Pedro Noguera and Robby Cohen ("Educators in the War on Terrorism"), Deborah Meier ("On Patriotism and the Yankees: Lessons Learned from Being a Fan"), Bill Bigelow ("Patriotism Makes Kids Stupid"), William Ayers ("Hearts and Minds: Military Recruitment and the High School Battlefield"), Chester Finn, Jr. ("Teaching Patriotism—with Conviction"), and Studs Terkel ("A Small Space of Sanity").

White, Edward G. *The Constitution and the New Deal.* Cambridge, Mass.: Harvard University Press: 2000.

Youth's Companion. "American Department: Preliminary Expense to April 1." A one-page accounting sheet summarizing expenses and receipts, including "Net Profits on 1908 Flags." No date. FJBP

———. "The Youth's Companion Flag Pledge," leaflet, 3 pages, no date. "Copies of this leaflet may be had by addressing The Department Editor, The Youth's Companion, Boston, Mass." FJBP.

———. "Preliminary Reading for Columbus Day," one-page printed, with illustrations, newspaper style. The National Public School Celebration of Columbus Day, October 21. Stories include "The Map Columbus Used," "The Ships of Columbus," and "Portraits of Columbus." Also includes

"The Public School Map," a state-by-state breakdown of the number of public schools and number of students. FJBP.

———. Issues of *Youth's Companion* from 1831. Available at http://books.google.com/books?id=SAM0AAAAYAAJ& printsec=frontcover&source=gbs_v2_summary_r&cad=0#v =onepage&q=&f=false.

Zeiger, Susan, "The Schoolhouse vs. the Armory: U.S. Teachers and the Campaign Against Militarism in the Schools, 1914–1918." *Journal of Women's History,* Summer 2003.

INDEX

INDEX

INDEX

INDEX

INDEX

INDEX